P9-DWK-890

FRANZ KAFKA

A *Study of the Short Fiction*

Twayne's Studies in Short Fiction

Gordon Weaver, General Editor
Oklahoma State University

FRANZ KAFKA

FRANZ KAFKA

A Study of the Short Fiction

Allen Thiher
University of Missouri–Columbia

TWAYNE PUBLISHERS • BOSTON
A Division of G. K. Hall & Co.

Twayne's Studies in Short Fiction Series No. 12
Research Assistant to Allen Thiher: Laura Anderson

Copyright 1990 by G. K. Hall & Co.
All rights reserved
Published by Twayne Publishers
A division of G. K. Hall & Co.
70 Lincoln Street, Boston, Massachusetts 02111

Copyediting supervised by Barbara Sutton.
Book production by Janet Z. Reynolds.
Typeset in Caslon 540 by Compset, Inc.

Printed on permanent/durable acid-free paper
and bound in the United States of America.

Library of Congress Cataloging-in-Publication Data

Thiher, Allen.
    Franz Kafka : a study of the short fiction / Allen Thiher.
        p.   cm. — (Twayne's studies in short fiction ; no. 12)
    Includes bibliographical references.
    IBSN 0-8057-8323-7 (alk. paper)
    1. Kafka, Franz, 1883–1924—Criticism and interpretation.
    I. Series.
    PT2621.A26Z9316   1989
    833'.912—dc20   89-36964
                                                          CIP

3

Contents

Preface

Kafka's position in twentieth-century world literature is without parallel. He is the only writer in German to have influenced world literature in the way that Faulkner, Proust, and Joyce have done. He is in fact the first writer since Goethe to have achieved such recognition for works of literature written in German. Moreover, one can plausibly claim that Kafka has been the dominant influence in the shaping of our postmodern sensibility since World War II. His practice of writing has been the most important model for the creation of fiction in the United States, France, Germany, Austria, and for many writers in Latin America. Absurdist fictions, the practice of black humor, the reliance on the paradoxes of self-reference, the sense of loss and alienation that abounds in our postmodern fictional and real worlds, all of this is part of a legacy that Kafka gave contemporary writers, and one that they with open recognition have exploited to the fullest. Since World War II we have all come to recognize that Kafka's voice is the voice of modern man and woman overwhelmed by the laws of a technocratic society over which, it seems, we have little if any control.

Kafka's work is also unparalleled for the role that chance played in preserving it. It is almost an accident that his work exists today in its present form; and his reader should bear in mind that few of the works for which Kafka is most famous were published by him. This is true of his three unfinished novels—*Amerika, The Trial,* and *The Castle*—and of much of his short fiction; it is also true that Kafka oversaw the publication of his best known short stories—"The Judgment," "The Metamorphosis," and "In the Penal Colony," to name the most famous. Kafka asked his best friend, Max Brod, to destroy the manuscripts he had left with him—which of course was a paradoxical way to assure that they would survive. The reader must also bear in mind that it was only nine years after Kafka's death that Hitler came to power. Kafka's family did not survive the Holocaust, and without Brod's great labors most of Kafka's work would not have survived either. In this respect Kafka's work speaks with a kind of paradoxically ironic voice, gaining its full recognition after the Holocaust, and yet speaking from some point before the horrible event.

The distinction between the works Kafka did and did not publish is important. Editorial choices were involved in publishing the novels and short fiction from the *Nachlass* (the German word designating the posthumously published works). Many of the titles are inventions of Max Brod. And if one can only be grateful to Brod for his work, one must nonetheless respect the inevitable fact that many of the works of the *Nachlass* are simply not finished. In this study of Kafka's short fiction and parables I respect this distinction by first addressing the posthumously published stories and then the stories that Kafka did publish himself. Since this study of Kafka's short fiction is intended primarily for readers who will read Kafka in English, I should point out that the various English editions of Kafka that a reader may encounter often do not respect the distinction between works published by Kafka and works published posthumously. *The Complete Stories*, edited by Nahum N. Glatzer (which is not really complete), arbitrarily divides the works into longer and shorter stories, though it does mark with an asterisk the titles of those stories whose publication Kafka oversaw. The reader who wishes to read only what Kafka did publish himself and, equally as important, get a sense of the way Kafka organized his collections of short stories, might first turn to the volume bearing in English the rather confusing title *The Penal Colony*. In this volume Brod brought together in proper order all the work that Kafka personally saw into print. The reader can then turn to other volumes that were published by Schocken in order to read the stories that Kafka left unpublished at his death. In my references here, however, I usually refer to *The Complete Stories*, since this is the best single volume of Kafka's short fiction. And when referring to the German text I have used Paul Raabe's *Sämtliche Erzählungen*, the easily accessible Fischer paperback edition.

In the first chapter of this study I deal in general with the posthumously published stories and parables, or the short works of the *Nachlass*. After a discussion of motifs of travel and space, of metaphors for communication in a number of these fictions, I turn in the next chapter to considerations of some of the earliest work that Kafka published: "Conversation with a Supplicant," the brief texts of *Meditation*, and the first chapter of *Amerika*, the text called "The Stoker." In the third chapter the breakthrough story, "The Judgment," and "The Metamorphosis" take center stage. In this chapter I enlarge upon some of the themes of self-reference and paradox by showing how the tales of the *Nachlass* are often self-designating allegories that interrogate their own status as forms of communication. The next chapter explores Kafka's masterpiece "In the Penal Colony." I attempt to show here that it continues Kafka's parodistic portrayal of writing as a fallen activity at the same time I broach a discussion of Kafka's view of history. An understanding of his view of history as a fall is both presupposed by his view of writing and is a logical outgrowth of his view of writing as a forever failing attempt to find revelation of the law. The last two chapters mainly discuss Kafka's last two published collections of stories, *A Country Doctor* and *A Hunger Artist*. Each of these chapters concentrates on what I take to be the most interesting central concerns of the collections—the question of dream rhetoric in *A Country Doctor* and Kafka's view of art and the artist in *A Hunger Artist*. Where appropriate for the purpose of comparison I have drawn from texts other than those directly under discussion. I hope that the reader will find that I have provided some consideration to all of Kafka's most interesting short works—though it would require a book considerably longer than the present one to examine adequately all of Kafka's stories.

Anticipating the reader's interest in locating a central theme, I should like to point to a recurrent notion in this study: Kafka's stories, like his novels *The Trial* and *The Castle*, usually take the form of allegory. Through allegory Kafka demands that his reader look beyond the often bizarre manifest context of the stories and ask what kind of symbolizing process is at work in the fiction. Kafka's allegory obliges the reader to ask what can be known through allegory even as he forces the reader to ask if the allegory points toward some knowledge of salvation or some knowledge of a law that might offer salvation. The allegory that asks what one can know through allegory places readers, like some of the characters in Kafka's fiction, in a situation in which they wonder how they can know that they know anything at all. Kafka's characters, like his readers, are often embarking, then, on a quest in which they wonder if they know that they know, and thus the quest becomes the itinerary of infinite regress: how do they know that they know that they know ad infinitum. This quest is often not directly presented, but rather is signified by allegorical indirection. And this allegory also invites us to try out as many interpretive possibilities as we can in order to find some symbol that will fit the allegory and limit its meaning to one we can clearly "know."

Preface

But the allegory that questions our possibility of interpreting it will also make it most difficult to find any final certainty—for the very process of the allegory denies that final knowledge that certainty exists. Thus Kafka has invented for us the contemporary allegory par excellence: a self-referential symbolic form that symbolizes paradoxically its own incapacity to symbolize.

Allen Thiher

University of Missouri–Columbia

Acknowledgments

I have been granted permission to quote from the following material:

Gustav Janouch, *Conversations with Kafka*. © 1968 by Fischer Verlag G.m.b.H., Frankfurt-am-Main. Reprinted by permission of New Directions Publishing Corp. In Great Britain, reprinted by permission of André Deutsch, Ltd.

Franz Kafka, *The Diaries of Franz Kafka, 1910–1913*. Translated by Joseph Kresh, edited by Max Brod. Copyright 1948 and renewed © 1976 by Schocken Books, Inc. Reprinted by permission of Schocken Books, published by Pantheon Books, a division of Random House, Inc.

Franz Kafka, *The Diaries of Franz Kafka, 1914–1923*. Translated by Joseph Kresh, edited by Max Brod. Copyright 1948 and renewed © 1976 by Schocken Books, Inc. Reprinted by permission of Schocken Books, published by Pantheon Books, a division of Random House, Inc.

Franz Kafka, *Letters to Felice*. Translated by James Stern and Elizabeth Duckworth, edited by Erich Heller and Jürgen Born. © 1967, 1973 by Schocken Books, Inc. Reprinted by permission of Schocken Books, published by Pantheon Books, a division of Random House, Inc. In Great Britain, reprinted by permission of Secker and Warburg, Ltd.

Franz Kafka, *Letters to Friends, Family and Editors*. Translated by Richard Winston and Clara Winston. © 1958, 1977 by Schocken Books, Inc. Reprinted by permission of Schocken Books, published by Pantheon Books, a division of Random House, Inc. In Great Britain, reprinted by permission of John Calder, Publishers, Ltd.

Franz Kafka, *Letters to Milena*. Translated by Tania Stern and James Stern, edited by Willy Haas. Copyright 1953 and renewed © 1981 by Schocken Books, Inc. Reprinted by permission of Schocken Books, published by Pantheon Books, a division of Random House, Inc. In Great Britain, reprinted by permission of Secker and Warburg, Ltd.

And many thanks to the friends and colleagues who have read Kafka with me through the years. And the greatest thanks of all to my assistant, Laura Anderson, who, in helping me put all this together, has been more helpful than even she realizes.

Part 1

THE SHORT FICTION

The Posthumously Published Stories

Few of Kafka's posthumously published short stories and parables are as well known as the pieces he published himself, which is a sign of what a perceptive if overly demanding self-critic Kafka was. There are a good many of these pieces: Paul Raabe's German edition of the complete stories includes thirty-four texts from the *Nachlass*, and this does not include all the parables found in Kafka's *Notebooks*. Taken as a whole these texts, which include such major stories as "Investigations of a Dog" and "The Burrow," are an extraordinary collection of projects and parables, comic masterpieces and pointed investigations of the limits of art and knowledge. Along with the three major novels that Kafka never published, these texts raise the question of what we mean by completing a work, the question of the importance of giving a piece of fiction some sense of closure.

The question is all the more interesting because Kafka's work—in the sense that the text might bring to a close its quest for some meaning—constantly denies the possibility of closure. I emphasize that completion is not just a matter of achieving some arbitrary length; rather, it demands a sense of closure that either resolves, or at least gives some sense of direction to, the meaning that the fiction has been putting into play. Traditionally stories have contained a sense of closure, and if Kafka was able to publish relatively little in his lifetime, perhaps it is precisely because he could never find a way to deal successfully with tradition's demand for closure. And Kafka respected greatly, to say the least, the demands of tradition.[1]

Kafka was unable to finish his first novel, *Amerika*, though he did have an ending in mind for it. In the Nature Theater of Oklahoma where, beyond what Kafka was able to write on this subject, his hero was to find a "limitless theater," and there, a profession, freedom, support, his home—*Heimat*—and a place where his parents would be restored to him through paradisiacal magic. This description of the projected ending points to Kafka's wistful desire for closure in the form of what religious tradition would call parousia, or the final restitution of meaning and the full presence of all things in the plenitude of God

3

and his word, logos. If Kafka had a smile on his face when he told Brod about this ending, it must have been in ironic recognition that if he finished little, it was because any closure demanded much. Of course he did finish some stories, but it was often by allowing the final meaning to founder on some arbitrary judgment that leaves the text's allegory an open question, through an ending in irony that points to the impossibility of closure as the text's (ironically) final meaning.

In his presentation of the two versions of Kafka's "Description of a Struggle" Brod observes that this story, the earliest extant piece of Kafka's writing, is also the only great work of the *Nachlass* that is complete. The story exists in an A version and a B version; and it strikes me as odd to call a story that exists in two versions complete, although the so-called A version of the story is perhaps the only long text of the *Nachlass* that does have a sense of closure. But "Description of a Struggle" is sufficiently unique to merit some special attention: this early story is the only work in which Kafka achieves a sense of closure by embedding narratives within narratives. By bringing a series of embedded narratives to a close Kafka creates a rather mechanical sense of an ending, though not one that brings about a closure of meaning. Kafka's "Description of a Struggle" probably defies any attempt at assigning a final sense to its bizarre series of narratives, unless perhaps we see the title as referring to the story's enactment of a struggle to narrate a closed text.

The tale begins when a first person narrator, finding himself in a Prague salon, meets a friend who might well be taken as a double for the narrator—a positive double who has the success with women that the narrator might like to have. The friend has a fiancée and has no trouble attracting the servant girl who kisses him as he and the narrator go out into a winter night in Prague. The acquaintance is a happy man, hence he is a dangerous man—according to the narrator who sees himself in danger of being cut down by his friend in the street if the friend should find himself in the mood for such a thing. The narrator tries to flee, falls down, and becomes the first of Kafka's characters who wants to go forward but cannot get anywhere.

The narrator can, however, swim in the atmosphere. For a moment he floats free of space and time as he recalls love and suddenly knows the names of all the stars. But his friend pulls him back to the Prague reality from which he seeks to free himself. This leads to part 2, or what is entitled "A Joke or Proof that It's Impossible to Live," a title suggesting that it is impossible to swing free from the limits of contingent existence and soar beyond them. Part 2 is divided in turn into three sections, each of which keeps the tale going forward, even if the narrator is incapacitated by his fall. To remedy his injury the narrator leaps on his friend's shoulders and in part 2:1, or "A Ride," he falls down with his friend who, it appears, now has a wound on the knee. The hidden wound will recur in Kafka's work as an image of the body's fallibility, but "A Ride" is probably the only story in which a character calls down a few vultures to keep company with the wounded.

With this macabre gesture the narrator can attempt to keep going forward in part 2:2, or "A Walk." This walk leads into a dream landscape that the narrator creates as he wishes. Using the power of language to confer being on whatever he says—at least in the narrative—the narrator self-consciously fashions the landscape he desires. Leading his character into a dreamscape, Kafka effects a psychological transition from the outer empirical or referential world of Prague to an inner or subjective world. It is like a dream world, one of the many Kafka explores in an attempt to find a way beyond the limits of fallen objective reality: "I reflected on why I had come here into this land whose ways [*Wege*] I didn't know. It seemed to me as if I'd gone astray here in a dream and understood the terrifying nature of my situation only upon awakening."[2] Kafka is not a complacent surrealist for whom dream is the road to the revelation of truth. Dream ways can lead one astray as well as to discoveries or revelations.

The narrator recognizes that he has entered a realm that, as he says, may be that of the imagination (*Einbildung*). To the second narrative scene Kafka adds a third when he leads his narrator along a way that goes to the river of part 2:3. Here he meets a character who seems to have escaped from Lewis Carroll and Alice's Wonderland: he is the Fatman. This corpulent character who takes over the narration, gives his name to part 2:3; this section is in turn divided into four subsections, so to speak, starting with part 2:3:a, or "An Address to the Landscape." Putting narrative boxes inside narrative boxes, Kafka takes a narrative way that seems increasingly comic in its proliferating incongruity. The fatman is carried into the river on a litter by his bearers who then promptly drown. The fat narrator floats down the river, a body turned loose on the flow of narration (the body seems to acquire a certain transparency at the end of the "Address" since a little seagull flies through the fat man's stomach).[3] A narrative voice that is out of control, the fatman begins his tale in part 2:3:b, or a "Conversation with a Supplicant"—a piece Kafka published separately and to which

I shall return in the next chapter. The supplicant also has a narrative voice that adds to the chorus when the fatman tells a tale of how he once asked the supplicant why he prayed by beating his head on the church's stone floor. The embedding of narrative voices continues in part 2:3:c and 2:3:d, with "The Supplicant's Story" and "Continued Conversation between the Fat Man and the Supplicant." A victim of the vengeance of "things," the fatman undergoes his demise in Part 2:4, on a page bearing the Nietzschean title of the "Untergang des Dicken"—or, literally, the going-under of the fatman.

The reader should, if possible, also recall at this point that the fatman's drowning is the end of a joke whose point was to prove that it is impossible to live. The fatman goes under, but going under is also the condition for the hero's survival or higher existence as described by Nietzsche, the philosopher who probably had the greatest influence on the young Kafka. It would be hardly incompatible with Kafka's sense of humor to see a Nietzschean superman in his drowning fat man. In any case, the narrator, having also experienced a great deal of fun, suddenly finds himself endangered by the dream-instability of his world: in anguish he finds his body changing size.

These narrative pyrotechnics, worthy of Lewis Carroll, come to a sudden end when, in part 3, the narrator finds himself again with his acquaintance in Prague. Is this an awakening or a forced return to some empirical reality? The narrator continues his conversation. His acquaintance boasts of his passions, though he regrets his love; finally he accuses the narrator of being a common man, incapable of love, only able to experience anguish. Like all of Kafka's heroes, the narrator knows he should think about getting married, so he replies that he does have a fiancée. And in response the friend sticks a knife in his own arm. The narrator binds the wound, though, absurdly enough, he happily maintains that the friend has inflicted the wound on himself for the narrator's sake.

One might say that at the end the narrator and his double have reversed roles. In the first part of the story the narrator imagines that his friend sees him going forward in stumbling motion, as a stick on which is awkwardly impaled a yellow-skinned and black-bearded skull. At the end the narrator's invention of a fiancée allows him to dominate his sexually potent friend. I leave to the reader's imagination what kind of interpretation the psychoanalytically inclined critic might make of the knife and the self-inflicted wound. Any such interpretation would be right to emphasize the fear of sexuality and the visions of mutilation that one can find in much of Kafka's work, and this fear is often what marriage entails. What is different about this earliest surviving piece of Kafka's writing is that it tries to make pure "narrativity" and complications of narrative structure carry the work forward to a final closure. Putting narratives within narratives, Kafka produces an artificial and even incongruous sense of ending merely by closing off the narrative proliferation. And if there is any sense in the "struggle" of which this is a description, perhaps it resides in Kafka's struggle to keep it all under control. Sexuality and narration are both difficult to handle because neither wish to be contained.

In its proliferation of narrative paths the "Description" also presents the earliest search for the kind of self-descriptive metaphor that will characterize much of Kafka's later work. The description of a walk, of a trip (perhaps a float trip), or the description of the search for ways forward, suggests metaphors for the story's own progress toward some impossible closure that would offer a final meaning or illumination, some definitive knowledge as to what the trip or the way is about. With this interpretation in mind in the rest of this chapter I should like to proceed with a general discussion of the stories and parables that make up the rest of the *Nachlass*. One should also bear in mind that, with the exception of "Wedding Preparations in the Country," written in 1907 and 1908, all of the remaining texts of the *Nachlass* were written after Kafka made his so-called breakthrough in writing "The Judgment" in 1912. In other words, throughout his life, often during periods of great creative intensity, Kafka wrote texts that he did not publish.

As I have said of "Description of a Struggle," one way to interpret these often enigmatic pieces is to view them as allegories about the story's own functioning. A text's function is to communicate a message or perhaps some form of knowledge over a distance, from some sending source to some receiving source. Little narrative complication is involved in these later tales and parables, for they are usually rather straightforward descriptions of some attempt to travel, to go through some space, or to reach some goal where one might give or receive some information, as, for example, at the end of some kind of a scientific investigation. In any case, the search for ways (*Wege*) is most often at the heart of these self-referential allegories that show Kafka to have been committed to the most basic questioning that modern man or woman can undertake.

In the case of a short text like "The Bridge" (1917) the allegory is comically transparent, since the narrator himself, stretched out as a bridge, is the way one is to take: his body is the space to be crossed. He is, as information theory might put it, the "contact" or the physical channel that provides the means for traversing the space that would lead from point A to point B; and much of Kafka's fiction is, at the most literal level, simply a description of how one might get from point A to point B. This can be a most difficult task, as in "The Bridge," for when a message-traveler steps on the narrator, he causes the narrator to fall into the depths. With the narrator's fall, the reader sees that a good many messages destroy the channel for communication, including, perhaps, the one the reader confronts on the printed page. Or, at the very least, messages go astray, as in "The Hunter Gracchus." In this story an allegorical voyager travels for all eternity, a wandering text as it were. Through no fault of his own he has been excluded from the beyond, and like an often interpreted text, passing from hand to hand, he sails from port to port, looking for an end to his trip that might be like a closure to a text: some anchored meaning, some securely communicated knowledge, or perhaps a final transcendence.

Distances often seem too great ever to be negotiated in these stories, like those spaces investigated by the narrator in "The Great Wall of China" or the distances from the borders to a fictional town in "The Refusal." In this latter story the town is too far from the capital for messages to arrive, and thus dynasties can go under without the news coming to the community. What does manage to cross spaces and get to the city are petitions to the courts—all of which are regularly rejected. This procedure generates constant traffic, an uninterrupted coming and going, as people come to the court seeking to encounter the law. They are never disappointed in that they can securely count on being refused this contact. All petitions are always denied. Judicial refusals do not stop movement, however. On the contrary, the regularly denied access produces a constant movement, a *gehen*, toward the certain denial. Refusal can produce certainty as much as can access, and this is the negative certainty that underwrites many of Kafka's communications about missed encounters with the law.

In "The Refusal" the fate of the message, the goal of the trip, is certain, which offers an ironic closure to the search for communication. Although nothing will become of the message when it has been received, it is certain that the goal of delivering the message is certain to be fulfilled. Such negative certitude is not a necessity, however, and often the goal of the trip is merely, as the brief text "The Departure" succinctly says, "just out of here"—"nur weg von hier." In the prototypical "Advocates" the narrator runs blindly through passages in what may (or may not) be a law court. His goal is to find some representative of the law, or advocates, but he encounters mainly old women. Yet he does not dare to turn back, for it would be unbearable to admit that the trip might not reach a goal:

> So if you have started out on a walk, continue it whatever happens; you can only gain, you run no risk, in the end you may fall over a precipice perhaps, but had you turned back after the first steps and run downstairs you would have fallen at once—and not perhaps, but for certain. So if you find nothing in the corridors open the doors, if you find nothing behind these doors there are more floors, and if you find nothing up there, don't worry, just leap up another flight of stairs. As long as you don't stop climbing, the stairs won't end, under your climbing feet they will go on growing upwards.[4]

Here the reader lays hold of one of the basic rules of Kafka's textual games that was only implicit in "Description of a Struggle": forward motion generates the spaces to be filled by that motion. This motion points in addition to the power of mere "going" to generate the metaphors that in turn appear to valorize the going itself, whatever be the (usually impossible) goal of the movement. In a sense, this movement is nothing other than the movement of language itself and its capacity to enter into an infinite metaphorical play. Language allows everything to be compared with everything, as in "Advocates"; steps are a metaphor for a possible transcendence, whereas, conversely, transcendence is a metaphor for steps, and both figure a movement toward meaning and a desire for closure. And the play of metaphor could continue indefinitely.

Once readers set this reading in motion, they can follow it through the *Nachlass* and beyond, like Sancho Panza following his horse-riding demon in the short text that reveals the truth about Don Quixote's travels. I shall follow this demon in later chapters, but here let us now pursue a reading of the *Nachlass* in order to see how travel is a metaphor for communication, communication a metaphor for travel, and how both travel and communication are metaphors for the work of metaphor itself.

In order that messages arrive, a space must be traversed, and a space traversed can be a form of communication. This movement is in turn a way of describing the existence of the text itself as a metaphor for a communication that goes to some problematic destination. There is, however, nothing extraordinary about this play of metaphor. It is part of "A Common Confusion," to cite the title of a piece in which the most daily transactions founder upon the impossible negotiation of the space-time complex that every traveler, like every message, must cross for business purposes (429).

Through this daily confusion, in texts like "The Problem of Our Laws" or "The Great Wall of China," Kafka's stories ask if there is nonetheless a law that regulates these metaphorical series of exchanges. Kafka's texts may abolish the distinction between tenor and vehicle in making metaphorical transfers, but the texts also ask if something other than gratuitous couplings is at work when language creates a world. Is it sufficient, for example, merely to drop the word "like" that creates a simile in order to make, metaphorically and arbitrarily, anything *be* anything else? If it is a basic rule that Kafka's texts generate spaces that the text's movement then has to fill, can one also speak of some law that arises from this repetition? Kafka's obsessive concern with laws or the law in general arises here as a question as to the nature of the linguistic transformations that we saw in "Description of a Struggle." Can language and its messages be subject to order, regularity, codes, in short, to some law governing messages and their travel?

This question folds back upon the text that asks it and becomes a question about the text itself. For metaphors also designate the story as a form of self-reflexive interrogation about the status of communication in the text itself. Kafka's allegorical self-doubling asks if the story itself has sent a message that someone might receive. This self-referential use of language creates many paradoxes. For example, the text as a metaphor is what it is, and yet it is something else. (The capacity for metaphorical transfer entails the possibility that language can propose that everything is what it is, yet is something else as well: Is Gregor Gregor or a vermin?) These paradoxes of self-referentiality mean that the text can send a message and yet prevent it from leaving, or make it stay at home at the same time as it travels forth. As a paradoxical traveler language can behave in the way the character Raban wants to behave in the *Nachlass*'s "Wedding Preparations in the Country." No willing traveler, Raban dreads his trip to the country and wants to stay at home. So he decides to resolve this conflict by behaving in an impossible, if metaphorical, way: Raban will stay at home and send his body on the trip.

> I don't even need to go to the country myself, it isn't necessary. I'll send my clothed body. If it staggers out of the door of my room, the staggering will indicate not fear but its nothingness. Nor is it a sign of excitement if it stumbles on the stairs, if it travels into the country, sobbing as it goes, and there eats its supper in tears. For I myself am meanwhile lying in my bed, smoothly covered over with the yellow-brown blanket, exposed to the breeze that is wafted through that seldom-aired room. (55–56)

This is a paradox only in a world in which metaphor does not invest all language. "Raban is a body" means that he can also not be a body, not be likened to this physical thing, and that, in fact, he can transform himself into anything, which, in fact, he does as he lies in bed: "As I lie in bed I assume the shape of a big beetle, a stag beetle or a cockchafer, I think" (56). Kafka's metamorphosis begins with the convertibility that metaphor inflicts on all things that are bound up in language, such as messages, texts, laws, and our very selves.

In sorting out these metaphoric transformations one constantly runs up against the undecidable nature of what is being transformed from what. One asks what is the primary meaning or the denotative value of terms, and what is the secondary or derivative use of words. In Kafka's garden of forking paths, to use the expression coined by the Argentine story writer Borges, there are only crossings and mixed breeds of words—*Kreuzung*—where language paradoxically seems to take two ways at once, producing the creatures that proliferate in Kafka's bestiaries. This is most explicit in "A Crossbreed" ("*Eine Kreuzung*" [a crossing in several senses]), a tale in which the narrator has an animal, half cat, half lamb, that he inherited, significantly enough, along with his father's possessions: "From the cat it takes its head and claws, from the lamb its size and shape; from both its eyes, which are wild and flickering, its hair, which is soft, lying close to its body, its movements, which partake both of skipping and slinking. Lying on the window sill in the sun it curls up in a ball and purrs; out in the meadow it rushes about like mad and is scarcely to be caught" (426). What can one do with such an undecidable creature, except attempt to decipher it and listen to its message: "Sometimes it jumps up on the armchair beside me, plants its front legs on my shoulder, and puts its muzzle to my ear. It is as if it were saying something to me, and as a matter of fact it turns its head afterwards and gazes in my face to see the impression its communication has made. And to oblige it I behave as if I had understood, and nod. Then it jumps to the floor and dances about with joy" (427). In this crossing one finds the emblem of the undecidable nature of metaphorical communication; the narrator can only act as if he had decoded the elusive message while wondering how he might dispose of this problematic creature.

Kafka's exploration of these metaphorical crossings leads (to use another metaphor) to increasingly random branchings and crossings, to increasingly comic undecidables. At the same time, however, his writings present an attempt to reduce these random ways, or *Wege*, to some kind of regular series. In a number of the texts in the *Nachlass* one finds a description of an effort to suspend the random branchings that the free play of metaphor introduces into these tales. These texts declare that the random must be unthinkable and that the undecidable must be eliminated. This refusal of the random can be likened to an epistemological axiom that certain narrators seek to oppose to the chance series that proliferate in Kafka's work. Often told by narrators who are quite conscious of undertaking research into causes and effects, these writings offer an introduction to what I would call Kafka's science: search or research that might discover some basic laws, if not the Law. Although these parables and descriptions are often caught up in the very randomness that they seek to abolish, these texts look nonetheless for certain ways and byways that might eliminate the random production of meaning that seems to be metaphor's distinctive capacity. For Kafka, as for moderns as diverse as Flaubert and Mallarmé, the elimination of the aleatory—of chance—is the first task of art. But only Kafka understood how comic this task can appear.

Consider in this respect "The Village Schoolmaster" (or, as it is also titled in translation, "The Giant Mole"). The object of investigation is a potential generator of metaphorical ways, a giant mole, a digger of burrows and labyrinths. In this tale, unlike the later "The Burrow," Kafka does not focus on burrowing, but rather on people's efforts to make sense of such a (metaphorical) beast—a purely contingent fabrication of language's combinatory powers. The great beast has not, it appears, received much attention from the authorities, for it has been left to an old village schoolmaster "to write the sole account in black and white of the incident, and though he was an excellent man in his own profession, neither his abilities nor his equipment made it possible for him to produce an exhaustive description that could be used as a foundation by others, far less, therefore, an actual explanation of the occurrence" (168–69). The old schoolmaster stands in an analogous relation to his discovery, as does every language user who must attempt, while forever lacking adequate means, to describe the inventions that language generates in its metaphorical explanations of reality. Giant moles infest our linguistic landscape in many guises.

Others may intervene, of course, to help us in our interpretive tasks, which is the role of the narrator who sets out to aid the old schoolmaster. The narrator attempts to communicate about the old man's communication, but metacommunication—or messages about messages—fares no better than first instances of communication in Kafka's writing. The narrator sends his report to the city, but naturally it goes astray. He sends a second report, but journalists assume that his second is only a repetition of the first and, in their common confusion, they dismiss it as a ridiculous redundancy. And if another report were sent, it would make little difference, as the narrator explains. Official science would take that report and make it disappear into the sum total of knowledge:

> Your discovery, of course, would be carried further, for it is not so trifling that, once having achieved recognition, it could be forgotten again. But you would not hear much more about it, and what you heard you would scarcely understand. Every new discovery is assumed at once into the sum total of knowledge, and with that ceases in a sense to be a discovery; it dissolves into the whole and disappears, and one must have a trained scientific eye even to recognize it after that. For it is related to fundamental axioms of whose existence we don't even know, and in the debates of science it is raised on these axioms into the very clouds. How can we expect to understand such things? Often as we listen to some learned discussion we may be under the impression that it is about your discovery, when it is about something quite different, and the next time, when we think it is about something else, and not about your discovery at all, it may turn out to be about that and that alone. (180)

This text, which is fundamental in illustrating Kafka's science, points to science—in the broadest sense—as an enterprise that masks the laws for random series while it constructs harmonious wholes that make the random disappear. The whole of science exists as that region of metacommentary that stops all self-reflexive questions and regress by absorbing all phenomena into a great metaphysical whole. Yet one can find little solace in science when one looks for a law for any particular series that one confronts. The closure of meaning can be achieved for totalities, but not for those specific giant moles that language serves up to us so often.

In a similar fashion one might consider the metaphorical mole narrator of "The Burrow" who, scientist that he is, fitfully entertains the idea of investigating the mysterious noise that he hears in his underground labyrinth. He knows that he should give himself over to research, dig more tunnels, traverse a space, and perhaps decode a noise that might be something other than a random sound. Such a "reasonable plan" for research, though never undertaken, does make us see that our constructions of scientific notions about causality are based on another metaphor. This metaphor draws together by association notions of travel and space, of distances traversed, as well as of points marking trajectories on the way that we then define as a causal chain. The narrator of "The Burrow" equates knowledge and science with the way he will dig in order to arrive at a goal, presumably the source of the noise, which is to say that he will construct the law of the series of disturbances that have entered the burrow. Yet the burrowing seeker of knowledge believes but little in his own plan, comes finally to understand it no longer, and, in any case, prefers to spend his time imagining random hypotheses about the noise. After all, if he were really to attempt to arrive at a knowledge of the noise, he might have to confront the possibility that he could be destroyed by his own discovery. An encounter with the law can kill as well as reassure, as more than one Kafkan character learns.

Literally and figuratively—and what exactly is the difference?—metaphors seem to generate laws that can impinge upon one's existence. If, for example, all are (like) dogs, then in this dog's life all should behave in accord with the law of dogs. Yet this generalization does not seem to hold true, and in "Investigations of a Dog" the (linguistic) law of the metaphor can be superseded by other laws. The initial law of dogdom does not hold unitary sway so that the law can explain the series of events that the tale's initial metaphor should generate. When some dogs begin to sing, for example, they provide another narrator-researcher with a matter for investigation, because these dogs clearly violate the law of their metaphorical dog existence:

Perhaps they were not dogs at all? But how should they not be dogs?
Could I not actually hear on listening more closely the subdued cries
with which they encouraged each other, drew each other's attention
to difficulties, warned each other against errors; could I not see the
last and youngest dog, to whom most of those cries were addressed,
often stealing a glance at me as if he would have dearly wished to
reply, but refrained because it was not allowed? But why should it
not be allowed, why should the very thing which our laws unconditionally command not be allowed in this one case? I became in-
dignant at the thought and almost forgot the music. Those dogs
were violating the law. Great magicians they might be, but the law
was valid for them too, I knew that quite well though I was a child.
(283)

And not only do they sing, these dogs walk upright on their hind legs.
A singing dog-metaphor walks and therefore violates the semantic and
biological laws of its own metaphorical being. For the nature of language use itself should seemingly guarantee codes and rules about
what is permissible in language and hence in the development of
metaphor.

The violation of these apparent laws generates the demand for more
science, since Kafka's axiom of knowledge is that there should be a
law that explains these series, a law of the deviant one might say, such
as for singing dogs that walk. As the tale itself claims, however, all
knowledge, the totality of all questions and all answers, is contained
in the dog. We can recognize the persuasiveness of this claim if we
again consider that in our self-enclosed world of language every metaphor, including singing dogs, can lead and connect to every other metaphor, through the passages provided by the infinite possibilities of
transfer and comparison.

The need for more science leads the canine narrator to other investigations. These dogs sing, an activity that in Kafka's world is associated with food. Music is a form of sustenance. So the music metaphor
leads to an inquiry about food, which, in turn, as the narrator knows,
will go astray in other metaphors:

I understand my fellow dogs, am flesh of their flesh, of their miserable, ever-renewed, ever-desirous flesh. But it is not merely flesh
and blood that we have in common, but knowledge also, and not
only knowledge, but the key to it as well. I do not possess that key

except in common with all the others; I cannot grasp it without their help. The hardest bones, containing the richest marrow, can be conquered only by a united crunching of all the teeth of all dogs. That of course is only a figure of speech and exaggerated; if all teeth were but ready they would not need even to bite, the bones would crack themselves and the marrow would be freely accessible to the feeblest of dogs. (291)

Finding himself going from knowledge to sustenance in this metaphorical transfer, the narrator first denies his metaphor, but only to go on and elaborate it. He wishes to find a "marrow that . . . is no food" (291). Yet he knows that this marrow, beyond being metaphorical sustenance, would be a poison born of an encounter with a law that no mere dog could endure (if such a law were to exist). Finally, it is as if Kafka were suggesting that in the curse of dogdom all we can bear is the random, that a vision of true necessity would, in its purity, annihilate us, and that science in any strict sense can only be tolerated so long as it remains a mythic provider of metaphorical sustenance.

One of Kafka's last works, "Investigations of a Dog" is perhaps the key text for exploring the ways that lead (or do not lead) to an encounter with a law that would reduce the random. Its central pages propose the most compressed demonstration of Kafka's science, the search for the knowledge of the impossible random series that might preside over the genesis of comings and goings, travels and passages, or the search for a closure of the open nature of the random. Moreover, the pages in which the dog-scientist laments the fall of his people can also serve as prolegomena to any science of history as well as to any history of science. Here the narrator claims that knowledge is increasing at an increasing rate among the dogs, though this acceleration can only be the measure of the fall from some time in some distant past when the "true Word" was on the tip of every tongue. But history is also a metaphorical way, a road leading from a crossroads, that has traversed a space between the present moment and the Word. The metaphor of the way designates history as another form of travel:

When our first fathers strayed they had doubtless scarcely any notion that their aberration was to be an endless one, they could still literally see the crossroads, it seemed an easy matter to turn back whenever they pleased, and if they hesitated to turn back it was merely because they wanted to enjoy a dog's life for a little while longer; it was not yet a genuine dog's life, and already it seemed intoxicatingly beautiful to them, so what must it become in a little while, a very little while, and so they strayed farther. (300)

The way from the crossroads has led to becoming dogs, which is a metaphor for the fall from Logos, the Bible's true Word, into a language ruled by the caprice of metaphor. The true Word would undoubtedly be a language without metaphor, without crossing paths, or a language without random, polysemous generating capacities. This would be the language of true science, of rigid laws and perhaps the Law, that could be spoken with a certainty that it would transparently illuminate our being. But such a language of necessary being can only be granted a historical existence, for what can bespeak its existence today, except mythic texts (like the Bible) whose need for interpretation quickly causes us to lose ourselves in the way of metaphor? In any case, the true Word would not speak of soaring dogs, of those *Lufthünde* whose multifarious activities violate our notions about both air and dogs. Yet once they are spoken, as the narrator says of himself, soaring dogs enter our language and become part of our picture of the world. What knowledge can one have of such a world in which the random couplings of language can exist with greater tenacity than our own doggy existence?

These are some of the riches to be found in what Kafka did not publish, in that laboratory of texts that only the vagaries of history have preserved for us. I now turn to those pieces of short fiction that Kafka himself deemed worthy of publication. With the axioms for reading furnished by these posthumously published parables and tales we can now follow the published work of a writer whose rigorous dedication to literature is almost without equal in our Judeo-Christian history.

First Publications

When we consider a few of Kafka's stories we encounter a kind of optical problem: we get double vision. We know today that the story or parable was published as a separate work but that it was conceived as part of a larger text that Kafka did not publish. As some of the stories were first written, they were embedded in a context larger than the one afforded by their isolated publication. And, as the French philosopher Jacques Derrida has observed about the parable "Before the Law," it is one text when it is read alone as published, and it is a different text when it is read as narrated by the priest in the church in the novel *The Trial*.[5] The words are the same, literally the same in each case, but they are framed in a different space and context, and, like different texts, they offer us different meanings. The Argentine short story writer Borges exploited this property—that language can remain the same while acting differently—when he created a short story in which his character Pierre Menard, a fictional French writer of the nineteenth century, rewrites *Don Quixote*, in Spanish, word for word. The novel written by the French symbolist writer is literally the *same* novel, but, as Borges ironically observes, much richer in meaning than the one written by a Spaniard in the seventeenth century. The seventeenth-century novel written in the nineteenth century is read in a context that generates far more complexity than did Cervantes's original novel.

Borges's imaginary rewriting of *Don Quixote* gives us the same novel libraries have always had on their shelves, and Kafka's publishing of "Conversation with the Supplicant" offered the world the same text it would have had, had he published "Description of a Struggle," except it is placed in a different context, which allows the story to have different meanings. As published in the literary review *Hyperion* in 1909, "Conversation with the Supplicant" is no longer embedded in the narrative within a narrative; rather, it presents a fairly straightforward first-person narration in which a neutral "I" describes the curious behavior of a young man who beats his head on his hands, which are stretched out before him on a church floor. Published alone the narrative shifts its focus from the narrator—our fatman who does not really appear as such now—to the solitary figure whose prayer seems to demand some kind of explanation. The reader who recalls the famous line from Kafka's Notebooks to the effect that literature is a form of prayer, or remembers that Kafka told Gustav Janouch that poetry tends toward prayer, will suspect that prayer is not an indifferent activity for Kafka.[6] Prayer is in several senses an image of the striving of literature itself. And if pounding one's head on the ground does not seem to be the most likely way of communicating one's desire for the sacred, who is to say literature is any more effective?

It is important to note that this masochistic scene is viewed by a narrator who, no longer possessed of his fat, is nonetheless the same narrator who comes to the church to delight in observing his girl at worship. His delight in such pleasures is a sign of his belonging to that well-assured world where men do not ask many questions. Such men accept the world as it is: they eat steaks and get married. But the view of the supplicant is enough to bring the narrator to question his assumptions—or at least to question the supplicant. He obliges the supplicant to admit that his form of prayer is less than noble in its motivation, for the supplicant tells him: "don't be angry if I tell you that it is the aim of my life to get people to look at me."[7] One might conclude that Kafka has given us a version of the supplicant as a primitive narcissist, and by implication, a self-referential commentary on the work itself as a form of exhibitionistic prayer (though I am not sure whether this commentary would apply best to the "Conversation" alone or perhaps to the entire "Description of a Struggle").

The tale's development, however, delightfully complicates this first approach to finding a context for the supplicant's whacky behavior, for the narrator himself offers his own, rather whacky interpretation of the supplicant's problem when he tells him: "It's a condition in which you can't remember the real names of things and so in a great hurry you fling temporary names at them" (PC, 13). It is hardly likely that any reader anticipated such an interpretation transforming the supplicant's "problem" into a problem with language. The narrator claims that the supplicant verbally transforms poplar trees into the Tower of Babel and flowers into the prototype of all exhibitionism, into Noah exposing himself when he was drunk. The supplicant replies, in an answer that probably anticipates reader response, that he is thankful that he does not understand what the narrator is talking about, which the narrator believes is denied by the very fact that the supplicant has spoken to him.

Kafka's work often keeps readers off balance with a mixture of parody and near-parody that suddenly seems to open up a world of authentic anguish (though Kafka's comedy is often the best expression of controlled anguish in literature). Off balance but wanting an explanation, readers find that they must engage in hermeneutics, to use the term that both religious and literary scholars use to designate their doctrines for interpretation. The need to interpret the grotesque image of a man praying with his skull converges with other questions that the "Conversation" brings up, such as why does one interpret, and, finally, what does it mean to drag one's body through a world in which one believes that one is only barely alive? Or, as the supplicant admits: "There has never been a time in which I have been convinced from within myself that I am alive. You see, I have only such a fugitive awareness of things around me that I always feel they were once real and are now fleeting away" (*PC*, 14). With double vision readers know that this confession is embedded in a joke that proves it is impossible to live; but in the context of the isolated tale it seems more likely that readers will see a kind of outcry, a demand for a world with a center, a sense of weight to it, what a contemporary writer like Peter Handke calls the weight of the world. The free-floating net of language that the narrator describes when he describes the supplicant's condition cannot give a center to the world, and thus the supplicant feels he has no ties to the world. He feels nearly invisible, ashamed when he faces others, and in his furtiveness he must "flit along the house walls like a shadow with hunched shoulders, many a time disappearing from sight in the plate glass of the shop windows" (*PC*, 15). This is a Kafkan joke, or an image of a life that is dead, or both—depending on the interpretive framework one uses.

The world in which life is impossible is moreover a scandalous place. Buildings collapse. People die on the street. The supplicant cannot understand how anyone can live in this world: "The air in the square is swirling about. The tip of the Town Hall is teetering in small circles. All this agitation should be controlled. Every window pane is rattling and the lamp posts are bending like bamboos. The very robe of the Virgin Mary on her column is fluttering and the stormy wind is snatching at it. Is no one aware of this?" (*PC*, 16). In lamenting that he is the only one to be afraid, the supplicant presents a comic image of the desire to control everything. His is a state of adolescent paranoia in which he is the only observer to understand the malign workings of the universe; or, in a slightly different frame of reference, he demonstrates Mel Brooks's sense of high anxiety—the compulsion to control a world that is predictably and comically forever out of control.

For the paranoid observer there are no neutral or indifferent phenomena in the world. And one way to prove this lack of indifference is to show that everything has meaning, which is another side of the desire to control everything. Language offers perhaps an illusory form of control, but to invest everything with a meaning promises minimally a control over the language that endows things with meaning. This is all a very circular state of affairs. Moreover, signs at best give one the power to control other signs, which send one searching ad infinitum for other signs and their meaning. But there are no events in the supplicant's world, as in the world of many of Kafka's characters, that are not also signs, potentially full of meaning. Once, for example, when the supplicant was a child he awakened and heard his mother call up to ask "what are you doing, my dear?," and a woman answered, "I'm having tea." The supplicant offers this banal event to the narrator for commentary or interpretation.

Our narrator first does not understand what the supplicant is aiming at, but finally dismisses the event as meaningless, as a "natural incident." This may well be the last time a character in Kafka's fiction finds that an incident is natural, hence meaningless, for in his desire for meaning the supplicant illustrates one of the central directions taken in Kafka's work: the world is an infinitely expanding realm of signs that promise that everything has a meaning even as the continued expansion assures that we shall never know what it is.

If literature is prayer, then, finally, this "conversation" has also been one of Kafka's. And a brief biographical excursus about the supplicant's astonishment about a natural event shows this to be true in a rather literal sense. In a letter that Kafka sent to Max Brod, dated 28 August 1904, he included the same trivial but potentially significant anecdote that the supplicant narrated to the uncomprehending narrator. Kafka wrote that one day, when he opened his eyes after a short afternoon nap and was not yet quite "certain about his life," he heard his mother call down from a balcony, "What are you doing?" and then a woman called out from her garden, "I'm having tea on the grass." Much like the supplicant, Kafka goes on to say, "I was astonished about the firmness with which men are able to bear life."[8] To read Kafka's letters as a parallel text to his stories does not offer any keys for their interpretation. The letters show that Kafka, who said that he was nothing but literature, could only write from a sense of astonishment, one that gave rise to anguish and laughter in equal measure in letters and fictions. If any insight into Kafka's work is to be gained by appeal to his biography, it is perhaps precisely this: Kafka's astonishment before the banally real motivated his behavior as much as his writing.

Kafka published other excerpts from "Description of a Struggle," both Version A and B, in periodicals before he gathered some of these together with other short pieces and published his first book, *Meditation*, in 1913. In all, this book includes eighteen brief texts that one can also find in *The Complete Stories*, though not in the order in which Kafka arranged them for publication. Arguments have been offered to the effect that the order has a meaning in reinforcing the themes. I am not personally convinced that reading these brief poetic texts in the order of Kafka's presentation greatly enhances the reader's appreciation of them, though one can turn to the English collection entitled *The Penal Colony* to find *Meditation* and the order that Kafka and Brod came up with, apparently on the very night during which Kafka made the acquaintance of Felice Bauer, the woman who was twice to be his fiancée.

I say that the order of the collection is of secondary importance because each of these "meditations" strikes me as a self-contained, singular crystallization of awareness or a discrete revelation. The reader finds here a mixture of parables, poetic prose, and enigmatic descriptions, as well as some good examples of Kafka's comic paradoxes. The variety of narrative techniques—memory and recall, neutral first person narrative, objective and hypothetical descriptions—point to the young Kafka's search for ways of narrating objective vision from a subjective point of view and at the same time his temptation to have recourse to the atemporal stance of the parable form that seemingly speaks the eternal truth of common experience.

There were few contemporary reviews of this little book, though the novelist Robert Musil did perceptively note in a review in 1914 that Kafka used a narrative style that blurs the distinctions between mental events and external reality.[9] The truth of this observation can be shown by turning to the work's shortest text, "The Trees." It can be easily quoted in its entirety: "For we are like tree trunks in the snow. In appearance they lie sleekly and a little push should be enough to set them rolling. No, it can't be done, for they are firmly wedded to the ground. But see, even that is only appearance" (382). Kafka begins the text with a "we" that asks us to grant some objective status to the comparison that the text proposes. Yet it is not clear who is speaking and from where the text's voice comes. Is the reader to take the comparison of mankind to trees as something made obvious by our common experience, or is this a revelation granted to a privileged observer? The text's final imperative "see" appears to establish a dialogue between an observer, with his special experience, and a listener, though the command to see could also be taken as a kind of objective form of exhortation, much like a set of instructions. Kafka's stance is often ambiguous; his style allows a poetic play of possibilities as in this suggestive little paradox about appearances.

The subject matter and themes found in *Meditation* are greatly varied, if not disparate, but our reading of the *Nachlass* has foreshadowed the one commonality that is present in most of them; the texts, whatever their context, usually describe some type of motion or renunciation of motion. They oscillate between presenting enactments of motion—walking, running, going on a trip—and the failure of movement. There are three notable exceptions to this pattern, I think, and these three texts all deal, implicitly at least, with women. I shall return presently to these three texts. With regard to the motif of motion, at this early stage in Kafka's career it does not seem to be so heavily invested with the metaphorical or allegorical values it acquires in later stories. (It is important to bear in mind that the pieces in *Meditation* were written before nearly all of the stories and parables of the *Nachlass*, as well as before the rest of the published work.) The typical configuration in *Meditation* is the enactment of a symbolic explosion, of a rupture expressing a desire to break out and go elsewhere. This desire for rupture has its roots, to be sure, in the romantic's refusal of the present world as well as the symbolist's desire to find access to a realm transcending the world of bourgeois fallenness. But *Meditation* is far more than a period piece rooted in the nineteenth century. In their exploration of paradox these texts are also the first steps toward the creation of our contemporary sensibility.

It is difficult to call most of these pieces fully developed stories, since as open-ended expressions of rupture and flight they are often poetic texts that lack the development and closure we normally attribute to the short story. For example, the opening text, "Children on a Country Road," is centered on a scene of nocturnal running. A first person narrator remembers running with his friends, with their "heads

full tilt into the evening" (380). In this disjointed piece the narrator
actually runs full tilt into a parable of sorts, for the child's goal turns
out to be that "city in the south" where one is never tired. One is never
tired there, we learn, because fools live there, and how, the text asks,
could fools get tired? This fragmentary narrative paradoxically undermines the desire for movement that it enacts when it proposes as its
goal that region where movement could continue forever—the land of
fools. Only fools would never grow tired of the running movement that
sweeps the children through the story and into the night. "Children on
a Country Road" opens *Meditation* with the paradoxical sense of irony
that we take to be the hallmark of Kafka and the Kafkan legacy.

The title of the second piece, "Unmasking a Confidence Trickster,"
sounds as if it might also apply in a self-referential way to Kafka. It
offers the reader a narrator who wants to go to an evening gathering
but is hindered on his way when he realizes that his companion is one
of the confidence tricksters he has heard about. The companion is literally a *Bauernfänger,* and the German word suggests that he preys on
peasants, or raw hicks. Despite this sudden revelation, the narrator
does not go on to tell what his dubious companion intends; rather he
proclaims, with typical Kafkan paranoid hyperbole, that *Bauernfänger*
are everywhere. He has met many of them and learned much from
them. And they have been constant impediments attempting to prevent "us" from getting to where we are trying to go. The narrator introduces the first person plural "we" in the creation of a rather typical
form of Kafkan pseudo-objectivity; we are now all caught up in this
open allegory in which we are invited to add whatever interpretive
elements we need. We can add whatever it was or is that hinders us in
our motion forward to our elusive goals. Many are the *Bauernfänger* that
have caught us, poor inexperienced provincial negotiators of reality.

The allegory is open in the sense that it gives us one side of a symbolic structure that applies perforce to another one, to the metaphor
that makes of our life and the achievement of our goals a form of movement. In this hall of reflecting figurative mirrors any experience will fit
as the one symbolized once we accept the basic metaphor, one so basic
that it is hard to think without this metaphor. But the trickster in this
story may well be the play of metaphor itself; and once we recognize
it, we do indeed see that the play of metaphor is everywhere. And,
with the narrator, we can then move on to those drawing rooms that
are the goal of our evening's excursion.

Kafka's exploration of themes of movement and rupture is accompanied by narrative and stylistic experimentation. In "The Sudden Walk" he narrates in the second person to describe "your" explosive wish to stride into the world so that "you" might gain "your true stature." In "Excursion into the Mountains" he plays with making a positive notion out of a grammatical negation, for the tale expresses the wish to travel into the mountains with "nobodies" ("mit einer Gesellschaft von lauter Niemand . . ." [Raabe, 12]). There, the narrator says, we shall all break out into song. Grammatical negation is transformed into a society that can travel toward ironic self-fulfillment. In Kafka's work music—for which Kafka slyly boasted to have no ear—is always a sign pointing to a desire for spiritual realization.

The sardonic humor expressing the plenitude realized by nobodies is also present in the piece called "The Tradesman." This character complains of his worrisome life, but experiences an ecstatic transformation as he comes home and travels up in his building's elevator. On his knees he looks into the elevator mirror and commands himself to fly into an imaginary space where anything can happen. He can soar over Paris or, more darkly, rob an inconspicuous little man in a doorway. This flight into other worlds comes meekly to an end when his elevator travels end at his apartment door where he is greeted by ordinary domestic reality in the person of his maid. The way is, as the tradesman says, always too short.

"Passers-by" also uses second person narration, this time to express the state of fear that you feel when you are walking at night and you confront passersby in the street. As you move along, you frame quick hypotheses about those you encounter in the dark, an activity that enacts in miniature one of the basic principles of Kafkan narration: forward movement brings you to new realms of experience about which there is no certainty and for which you—character or reader—can only frame multiple and usually inadequate hypotheses.

Kafka's astonishment about mere being underlies the trip another narrator makes when traveling "On the Tram." This first person narrator looks at a young woman and wonders in amazement how, by simply being, "is it that she is not amazed at herself, that she keeps her lips closed and makes no such remark?" (389). Of course, one can be amazed at the mere fact of existing and want very much to be something else, as is the case with the one paragraph text, "The Wish to Be a Red Indian." Using the third person singular *man* (or "one") as a neutral subject, Kafka expresses the wish for the total rupture with existence that one would know if one were an Indian flying away on a rapid steed. There is here, to be sure, a kind of romantic desire to be "anywhere out of the world" (as Baudelaire put it), but Kafka's wish, with its ironic objectivity, has such a comic specificity to it that the reader quickly realizes there is a double meaning, in effect a critique of the very possibility of running away over the plains to wherever an Indian might run—perhaps to the Nature Theater of Oklahoma.

The renunciation of movement plays a role in fewer texts than does the wish for motion, and these pieces are perhaps most effective insofar as they set forth an ironic counterpoint with the texts of rupture. In "Resolutions" the narrator describes how he might lift himself out of a miserable mood. But the difficulty presented by the necessary movements, the impossibility of defying his own feelings, brings him to conclude that it would be best to sink into an inert mass. The final expression of this motionless state would be to limit oneself to the "characteristic movement" of running one's little finger along one's eyebrows. Life reduced to the motion of a little finger is the hyperbolic opposite of running away on an Indian pony. The same kind of immobility strikes the character of "Bachelor's Ill Luck," who remains unmarried; for Kafka, the perpetual bachelor, believed there was no fulfillment without marriage, and his narrator imagines what it would be like to lie ill in bed with no children: "That's how it will be, except that in reality, both today and later, one will stand there with a palpable body and a real head, a real forehead, that is, for smiting on with one's hand" (395). The locus for immobility is the palpable body on which the real announces its presence, often through a blow on the head or even the movement of a little finger. But if we think we have lost something in this immobility, we then learn in "Reflections for Gentlemen Jockeys" that there would be no point in winning our horse races, for we would merely expose ourselves to even worse fates: envy, anger, ridicule and isolation await the victor.

In Kafka's world one solution for the palpable body is for it to place itself by a window, the recurrent window that is the separating pane between inner and outer worlds. Sitting by the window the Kafkan character in "Absent-minded Window-gazing" gives form to a situation in which he remains immobile in his inner space while he looks out upon an unattainable outer space that one might yearn to traverse to find whatever it is that awaits one at the end of the impossible ride. As readers, what are "we" to do on this spring day? "You" go to the window and look at the setting sun, you see a girl strolling and then a man: "And then the man has passed by and the little girl's face is quite

bright" (387). Does this concluding line suggest that we have wit-
nessed some epiphany or revelation, or are we separated from essential
being by our immobility behind the window? Much like a Zen parable,
the text forces us to ask a question for which there is no immediate or
apparent answer. The window can separate the character from the
world, as in later stories such as "The Judgment" and "The Metamorphosis"; sometimes it can also draw the character into the world, as is
the case with the solitary narrator of "The Street Window." He may
refuse mobility: "And if he is in the mood of not desiring anything and
only goes to his window sill a tired man, with eyes turning from his
public to heaven and back again, not wanting to look out and having
thrown his head up a little, even then the horses below will draw him
down into their train of wagons and tumult, and so at last into the
human harmony" (384). The drawback may well be that the horses are
drawing him into human and *only* human harmony. In any case the text
claims that the window opening on the street is a necessity for the
immobile character who will not sink entirely into a morass of nonbe-
ing—whether there be a harmony beyond human harmony or not.

The three texts in *Meditation* that I see as dealing with women do
not directly present patterns of mobility and immobility. These pieces
are "Clothes," "Rejection," and, indirectly, "Unhappiness," with its
child-woman ghost. One might also include "On the Tram" in this
group, since in this story, and also in "Clothes" and "Rejection," Kafka
focuses on a woman and on the clothes she wears. In these pieces it is
clear that Kafka is fascinated with women and the sensuality that
emerges from their skirts, bodices, and lace.

With a bit of ingenuity one might argue that Kafka presents women
as impediments to motion, because they arrest the narrator's attention,
even if, as the title "Rejection" suggests, the woman encourages the
hopeful narrator to continue on his way home. In "Clothes" the narrator is stopped by the beauty of clothes whose besmirching he foresees
when he proclaims that sometimes at night when women come home
late from a party their faces, like garment-masks, appear to them in
the mirror to be worn out, bloated, covered with dust, seen by everyone and hence not wearable any longer. A woman's face is also a gar-
ment, one that can be filthied by the looks that others bring to bear on
it. Moreover, as Kafka's letters to Milena make clear, he had trouble
seeing sexual attraction as anything other than a defilement of the
wholeness of being. But sexuality is all-pervasive in Kafka's work. It
is a kind of snare that no Kafkan hero avoids, or perhaps really wants

to avoid, as one sees in the entanglements that eros creates in texts as varied as "The Judgment" or *The Castle*. Eros threatens the desire to move on and stay in motion.

These potential disruptions culminate, significantly enough, in the final meditation, "Unhappiness." This story opens with a wildly expressionistic image of the narrator running, within the confines of his own apartment, as if he were on a race track. Reminiscent of the Munch painting of the same name, a cry reverberates in the room, calling forth, "like a small ghost," a child who enters the room. The child is female (and in German she is a *Kind*, a term allowing more sexual overtones than "child"). The sensual suggestiveness continues when the narrator must "cover himself," since he is described in the German original as half naked—even though he says he has been expecting the visit. The reader is not too surprised then when the narrator tells his visitor, using the formal form that one reserves for adults, "Sie sind schon ganz erwachsen" ("You are quite grown-up") (Raabe, 20).

She does appear to be more adult than child in the encounter that gives rise to a rather comic series of retorts between the narrator and the female ghost who, we discover, is both a part of the male narrator's nature and totally other. The calling forth of the child-woman is part of a Kafkan vision of eros, in which the divided self perpetually founders on the unhappiness caused by its nature as an erotic being. The narrator tries not to let himself be ensnared by his visitor, but when he puts his feet in motion he trips over a cumbersome leg of a chair in a Chaplinesque fashion. Fleeing desire is hopeless.

His next attempt at leaving her is also interrupted, this time by a neighbor on the staircase with whom he must have a discussion about his visitor. The neighbor expresses skepticism about the existence of ghosts, to which the narrator replies that his not believing in ghosts is of little help when it comes to getting rid of the fear one might feel in their presence: "that's only a secondary fear. The real fear is a fear of what caused the apparition. And that fear doesn't go away" (394). Angst, anguish or dread, is more basic than any appearances; it underlies all other fears; it is the ground against which all stands out and takes on its appearance, as the philosopher Heidegger argued. Yet in Kafka's world nobody would be rid of this fear, and the narrator would be very angry with his neighbor if his neighbor were to take away the narrator's ghost.

One is wedded to one's anguish as one is wedded to one's (female) ghost, or to one's erotic nature, wanting to keep it and chase it away at the same time. This story illustrates one of the best examples of Kafka's short open allegory. It allows the interpretation of one or several basic experiences—eros, fear, anguish—showing their interrelations while it allows readers a kind of interpretive freedom to bring the story to bear on their own experience. The allegory presents a basic structure of experience; and in "Unhappiness" that structure is based on the comic dialectic of the impossibility of having a consistent desire.

Finding it difficult if not impossible to flee his ghost, the narrator gives up his attempt to go out and returns to his apartment to go to bed. That is a closure of sorts, though lying immobile in bed is no easy matter in Kafka's fiction. The question of closure is, however, one that haunts all of Kafka's writing like a ghost. And at the point in his publishing career to which we have come, the years 1911–12, closure was especially crucial. During this time he wrote most of his first novel, *Amerika*, of which he finally published the (completed) first chapter, "The Stoker," in 1913. During the night of 22 September 1912 he wrote the piece of short fiction that is usually considered his first major work, "The Judgment." This was his "breakthrough," by which I think we can understand that Kafka finally wrote a text that he could call complete, though he was not sure why himself. It is noteworthy that much of the writing of *Amerika* presumably preceded the so-called breakthrough (though "The Stoker" was written shortly after "The Judgment"). Before turning in the next chapter to a discussion of "The Judgment," I should like to conclude here with some considerations of *Amerika* and "The Stoker." The novel reflects some of the same themes that are found in "The Judgment" and sets forth a context that allows full appreciation of the closure that Kafka found for that short story.

In a sense "The Stoker," though a chapter of a novel, belongs to a discussion of Kafka's published short fiction, since it was published separately by Kafka (and Paul Raabe's edition of the short stories in German includes the chapter). For the moment, however, I prefer to consider it a first chapter of the incomplete novel and not to engage in a discussion of the interpretive frames one might take up. In a diary entry of 8 October 1917 Kafka saw "The Stoker" as the beginning of a novel that would have been a kind of contemporary imitation of Dickens. The novel narrates the adventures of a good-hearted adolescent protagonist, Karl Rossman, beginning with his arrival in America after he has been sent away from his German home for having impregnated a servant girl who had seduced him. *Amerika* begins in effect with a judgment and a sentence (which are the two meanings of the German term *Urteil* that is translated as "The Judgment"). Karl is condemned to exile to the mythic world of America, a world where, in Kafka's ironic perspective, fulfillment might be possible, if it were possible anywhere. Karl is another traveler, embarking on the impossible task of getting from point A to point B—point B being that marvelous Nature Theater of Oklahoma to which I have made reference.

What interests us here is less the theater of annunciating angels than the trip that Karl undertakes. Throughout *Amerika* Karl's voyage is set in motion by a series of judgments. It is a condemnation that sets his trip in motion and it is a series of negative judgments that keeps him moving toward no well-defined goal. After being rejected by his family, Karl is received, in quite wondrous fashion, by his successful uncle in New York, while witnessing aboard ship the trial and judgment of his new friend, the stoker. After a stay with his uncle, Karl is again condemned and banished when he unwittingly disobeys his uncle. Going to work for a hotel, Karl, a scrupulous employee of the most Dickensian sort, is accused through no fault of his own of thievery, disobedience, and drunkenness. He is, of course, found guilty and condemned to leave. A policeman in the street immediately suspects him of crime; and in the last chapter (before the fragment on the Nature Theater) Karl is virtually condemned to slavery by his former travel companions who use his suspected guilt to blackmail him and lock him up in an apartment where he must serve the voluptuous Brunelda.

Amerika has no closure, for, unlike the incomplete *The Trial* that nonetheless brings Joseph K. to a grisly final judgment, this novel could only end in a final judgment that would exonerate the forever innocent Karl Rossman—and there are no exonerations in Kafka. As a midwesterner I must express my great admiration for the impossible ending that Kafka's Nature Theater of Oklahoma promised—but there is no parousia on the plains. *Amerika*'s lack of closure is not unlike the lack of an ending for Kafka's final novel, *The Castle*; in both novels Kafka set himself the task of getting his hero to a goal that the novel is required to demonstrate as impossible, although the attempt in *The Trial* is more self-consciousness.

Max Brod says that Kafka published "The Stoker" in 1913 with no prompting from anyone, although it is also true that the publisher, Kurt Wolff, had asked for it after he found out that Kafka was working on a novel. I bring up the circumstances of publication because they point at once to Kafka's reluctance to publish and to his probable belief that "The Stoker" was sufficiently complete in itself to offer something that could stand comparison with "The Judgment." For it strikes me that "The Stoker" has a unity that makes it readable on its own terms (though the contemporary reader inevitably has a double perspective on the text).

It seems clear that "The Stoker" enacts a kind of mythical fall: Karl Rossman is driven from his home for having tasted forbidden fruit through no real fault of his own—and without even really experiencing the pleasure that sin offers. The analogy of the lost homeland to a possible paradise is underscored when Karl arrives at the harbor of New York where the Statue of Liberty is described, like an avenging angel, as holding up a sword above the arriving traveler. After that image one has no doubt that Karl has been permanently driven from the realm of innocence.

Karl is about to go ashore when he realizes that he has left his umbrella below deck. He goes below and embarks on a wandering in a spacial labyrinth that prefigures his later wanderings—and which is an elaboration of the basic Kafkan configuration of trying to get from point A to point B. Labyrinths, spacial and semantic, are the stuff of Kafka's fictions, and the mazelike bowels of Rossman's ship are another emblem of the space the hero and the reader would have to cross to get to a realm of meaning. Karl gets lost below deck and begins to hammer "like a madman" on a little door. Behind it he meets the stoker, a weak father image who might protect Karl or give him his place on ship—if the stoker were not soon to be on trial himself.

"The Stoker" ends with Rossman's new friend being brought before a court of sorts. The stoker makes a bumbling attempt to defend himself before the ship's captain against charges brought against him by the seemingly malevolent chief engineer. Karl's presence here is tolerated, though at first a servant tries to chase him out of the captain's quarters as if he were an *Ungeziefer*—or that vermin into which Gregor Samsa finds himself transformed in "The Metamorphosis." Karl Rossman is a prototypical Kafkan hero in that he has a sense of his innocence that any child in a Dickens novel might have and, at the same time, he is a vermin to be tolerated as a necessary evil. "The Stoker" ends with a certain ambiguity when Karl meets the rich uncle who seemingly promises to protect the young man. Yet, as Karl leaves the captain's room, he sees that he leaves the stoker, now more Karl's double than his protector, to face a long line of witnesses that the chief

engineer has called forth. The weak father image is going to be condemned, we feel, leaving Karl in the charge of a powerful figure who,
in Kafka's world, can only be a judge. (He is in fact called a senator.)
The judge will condemn in the name of a law that the condemned will
never know. Wandering in the labyrinth turns up a powerful father-
judge, but such travel never produces an encounter with the law he
enforces, the law that might illuminate the maze.

"The Judgment" and "The Metamorphosis"

Before turning to the two major stories of 1912, "The Judgment" and "The Metamorphosis," I should like to enlarge upon my discussion of Kafka's use of language to talk about language, or what is called metalanguage. This brief discussion should enhance an appreciation of these two stories as well as the rest of Kafka's work. To this end I shall consider a parable that Kafka wrote near the end of his life, in 1922 or 1923, and to which Max Brod gave the title "On Parables." The title reflects the fact that this is a parable on parables, or writing about writing, or more technically, a form of self-referential metalanguage. This parable about parables begins by noting that many complain of the uselessness of parables since, for example, when the writer or the sage tells us to "go over," he really has nothing precise in mind, and so a parable is of no use in practical life: "All these parables really set out to say merely that the incomprehensible is incomprehensible, and we know that already. But the cares we have to struggle with every day: that is a different matter" (457). But the parable goes on to say that a man once said that if we would only follow parables, then we would become parables and get rid of all our daily cares:

> Another said: I bet that is also a parable.
> The first said: You have won.
> The second said: But unfortunately only in parable.
> The first said: No, in reality: in parable you have lost. (457)

This is one of the most teasing pieces in Kafka's *Nachlass*, and I have never been sure that I really understand it, but if the following explanation is approximately correct, then I think that this parable tells us a great deal about the struggle Kafka faced in undertaking his major writings.

As any logician knows, self-referential language—language referring to itself—is full of paradoxes, not the least of which is that a sentence can deny its own truth value (compare "This sentence lies."). How can language deny itself? For Kafka this property is not just a logical dilemma, but part of the dilemma of literature. For literature, in order to justify its claims, must speak about itself, and how can it do so without falling prey to the paradoxes of self-referential language?

In the parable "On Parables" the reader finds statements about the nature of literary language of which the statements themselves are primary examples. At the same time that they are statements about themselves they are also statements of a general nature about all parables or literary language. The mind has a bit of difficulty holding together the way that all of this functions: ordinary statements that at one and the same time are examples of metalanguage and are self-referential and are thus examples of the demonstration that the metalanguage would undertake. In a sense this is then a logical set that includes itself as a member. This is a statement about statements that is a statement, which has something of the same logical structure as imagining the set of all houses and saying that it is a house. We are pretty certain that the set that includes all elephants is not itself an elephant, so, how, we ask, can the set of all parables be included somehow in a parable? It appears that this set within a set is logically impossible, a contradiction, and yet we know that we must talk about language sets within language and with language.

In its modestly self-referential way the parable about parables seems to assume the necessity of logical contradiction in one of the two realms in which we can run our lives—in reality or in the realm of logical purity. The latter includes a realm of literature where language would function with a kind of logical necessity of which poetry can only dream. One can guess that a parable is only a parable, which means that, as Kafka puts it, one wins in the realm of reality; here one deciphers that his parable's self-referential language is merely an example of paradox. But with that stance one loses in parable that realm of logical purity that one might inhabit if one were able to listen to that language that would take one beyond mere paradox and bring us to the realm of necessary language, of law beyond contradiction and interpretation.

I am not sure that this interpretation eliminates the paradox of the parable on parables, or if it merely deepens it; in any case, this explanation should point to the kinds of reading difficulties and pleasures readers face when they turn to Kafka's major pieces of short fiction (including a good many pieces from the *Nachlass*). Kafka's fictions turn back on themselves, so to speak, in that they are forms of autorepresentation that use the kind of metalanguage and self-referentiality I have just elaborated. His stories ground themselves not primarily in some representation of external realities, but rather in that they are mirrors of their own functioning. Or perhaps one should say they reflect their own dysfunctional nature as logical paradoxes.

To paraphrase what many critics have said about Kafka, it may well be true that his works are reflections of an absurd world in which the emptiness left by the death of God, as Nietzsche put it, has been filled by the creation of a proliferating state bureaucracy, but the power of Kafka's work really lies in its power to sabotage the possibility of making any such clear statement about it. The works' power lies in their undermining any clear representational system or systems of reference that lies beyond the text itself. These stories refuse the referential grounding one needs in order to generate sense, as they designate, often in parodistically fragmented ways, how the fictions these stories contain can only mirror themselves as they attempt to represent a world. Mimesis in the sense of a symbolic representation is not excluded from Kafka's stories, but it is subordinated to a system of self-reference that points to the near impossibility of symbolic representation. And, as I suggested earlier with regard to the *Nachlass*, it is this sense of literature as a necessarily self-designating construct that marks the extent to which Kafka's work ushers in the era of postmodern literary sensibility.

With regard to the published work, it is with "The Judgment" that Kafka's narration first clearly begins to designate itself as incommensurate with any transcendent space of discourse that might allow the genesis of meaning to take place. "The Judgment" sets the pattern for which the parable on parables comes as a kind of ultimate—I hesitate to say—logical conclusion; Kafka's work closes in upon itself and becomes a self-referential interrogation about the text's relation to any other realm. In this respect the story comes to refuse the essential revelation that it seeks—the revelation that has been the goal of most modernist texts, as well as the scriptures. Kafka's work becomes a consistent demonstration of the impossibility of finding plenitude through language. And when he gives up on finding the Nature Theater of Oklahoma, his work presents perhaps the most radical example of a truly secular literature, for it marks the end of the modernist quest for salvation through literature.

I wish to stress this point, for one could well ask how many modernists, for example, the early modernist Flaubert who had such a strong influence on Kafka, could be said to have a religious side. But my point here is that the very structure of meaning in both realist and later modernist fiction of the early twentieth century is grounded in terms of a religious model: meaning is the making manifest of an absent discourse. Meaning is produced when the text is, in effect, read in terms of a logos, to use the biblical term, that would be its origin. Logos, I recall, is the term designating language's power to confer being. This originating logos, or discourse, exists outside the story. Realism in literature means that "reality" is a discourse that must be made present. And the proper reading of realist fiction means we read beyond the text and look for another text beyond it, which we call the "real" text or world (though, as "On Parables" suggests, it is not easy to win at that game). Realism means a story reveals some privileged essence in language that exists nonetheless outside of language, that is, in the realm of the real (and yet can exist only in the discourse that reveals that essence). In later modernists, such as Proust and Joyce, the desire to reveal essence, or "epiphanies" as Joyce, with a full sense of his religious mission, called them, offers us a comparable structure: the absent essence can be made present through the structure of language.

The goal of these modernist fictions is the disclosure of what is otherwise absent, invisible, unmanifest. In Kafka's work, on the other hand, the stories, seemingly laden with metaphors and symbols, may appear to aspire to this revelation of an absent discourse, a revelation of the transcendent discourse that would endow the narration with meaning and perhaps bring about salvation. But his fictions contain inscribed within themselves recurrent indices that show that this fictional language is to be read self-referentially. This self-reference stops the reader from making reference to a transcendent discourse. In Kafka language is fallen logos. His language is also metalanguage about that fall as it turns in upon itself in lamentation or, equally often, in parody of its aspirations to be that logos that the Bible places at the origins of what is.

"The Judgment" was written in one feverish sitting—late one night in the fall of 1912, after Kafka had been working for some time on the novel now known as *Amerika*. Kafka felt that this work was a breakthrough in his writing, though I have noted that he was not entirely aware of why this was so. I would propose that it was in this story that Kafka first found, perhaps intuitively, the narrative patterns that would increasingly predominate in the later stories. In this story the reader confronts a narration inscribed with signs of its own inadequacy, though in no systematic way. Systematic self-mirroring, as in André Gide's *The Counterfeiters*, can be a modernist technique that reflects a modernist's belief in language's capacity to double itself as a fullness, even if the novel is a tale of failure. In "The Judgment" the very fragmented and diffuse nature of the self-representation is part of a strategy to narrate a story that contains within itself a representation of its own radical incommensurability.

The third person narration in "The Judgment" seems to coincide with the restricted field of consciousness of the protagonist, Georg, a young businessman who works with his father. The story appears to present an objective narration in which the representation given to the reader by a neutral or absent narrator seems to coincide with Georg's own representation of his situation. (The narrator is absent in the sense that he, she, or it is never *in* the narration.) This narrative point of view is the one that promises, perhaps falsely, that the reader is entering an ordered realm of discourse in which meaning is generated according to well-known models. One of Kafka's favorite strategies is to exploit this kind of narration that, after a century of realist writers, had come to be codified as a form of discourse that guarantees the truth and stability of the represented world at the same time that it seems to offer a transparency through which the absent narrator promises to make present an absent but anticipated otherness. In Kafka's story, however, this use of a received narrative technique is the first step in ordering a fictional world that turns against its certain or transparent meaning in an ironic reversal.

Kafka begins the story by presenting an image of writing, for Georg sits mulling over the possibility of writing to a friend in Russia about Georg's forthcoming marriage or about his success in business. On one level this writing could be nothing more than the communication of a message, of information sent across a vast space. That space in a literal sense is the vast plains of Russia, though on reflection the reader may suspect that this is a space that, like the great expanse of China in later tales, no message could ever cross. Kafka starts the story, then, with a reference to the space of communication, or that space of infinite loss in which all messages go astray. Writing in this space of ironic reversals never really aims at an outer world, but only designates itself and the space within which it is enclosed. As the rest of the story makes clear, Georg's letter can never be mailed.

With this reference to writing at the story's beginning Kafka has inscribed within his text a double for what the reader takes to be a story's usual function. Like a letter, a story should transcend its own ι nmanent space by performing referentially as a form of communica'ion. This doubling is underscored when Georg, having finished the diffi ult task of writing the letter, continues to sit at the table: "With the letter in his hand, his face turned toward the window, Georg had remained seated at the table for a long time. As an acquaintance passed by and greeted him from the street, he had barely answered with an absent smile" (modified translation of p. 80). The image of the window here, as in the stories we have already discussed as well as in "The Metamorphosis" and *The Trial*, appears as an image of the desired transparency, of the opening onto the world that would allow the genesis of meaning and a communication opening out of the text. The constant play between inner and outer space in Kafka's settings often stands as an analogue for the relationship between the narrative space within language and an extratextual space beyond the closed labyrinth of the narration. Georg, the writer who has now completed his narration, seems to have trouble at this moment establishing a contact with some "exteriority" beyond the space that contains him. The passing acquaintance whom Georg scarcely acknowledges would, in this perspective, be another double in this network of doubles, in this case it would be a double for the friend in Russia to whom Georg's letter is addressed. And the absent smile is another sign of the absence that permeates this paradoxical text; it would be the ironic smile produced by the impossibility of making contact through the window that is often a barrier, not a source of illumination in Kafka's world.

The darkness of the narrative space becomes clear, to use a Kafkan reversal, when Georg enters his father's somber room for the first time in months. The representation of his situation that Georg made in his letter is somehow not adequate to account for the way the story suddenly portrays the remote inner space where the father sits in a corner hung with mementos of Georg's dead mother. The narrative movement is again doubled here by the image of reading. The father scans a newspaper that he holds to one side in order to overcome a defect in his vision. Not only does the father have trouble reading, but he also eats with little relish. On the table stand the remains of the breakfast that the father has scarcely touched. Reading, especially reading newspapers, and eating or attempting to eat are recurrent motifs in Kafka's work, and their common presence in this first encounter with the father points to their doubling each other as emblems of sustenance. As a reader and as an eater the father initially seems inadequate. This impression undergoes an ironic reversal, for, if the father initially suffers from a weakness of vision, he can then claim superiority of insight when he imposes his interpretation of the family's situation on Georg.

In this first scene, however, the father is associated with the newspaper—an image of degraded language in Kafka's work—and with the sustenance he cannot ingest, with the food that the father, like Gregor Samsa or the later hunger artist, needs to stay alive. Deprived of meaningful discourse, incapable of nourishing himself, this sickly father is the first image of the interpreter of the law in Kafka's world.

Georg first confronts his father within the dark innerness of the house, which seems to double for the text's own enclosure. Here Georg learns that, according to his father's interpretation, Georg has completely misrepresented his situation to himself and to others. The paternal reversal begins when Georg tries to cover up the old man in bed—he wants to *zudecken,* and the verb here suggests that he might be attempting to conceal or to hide the father and hence the interpretation that condemns Georg's representations and writing. Suddenly the old man leaps up and, demonstrating his surprisingly superior strength as well as his interpretive skills, proclaims that Georg's marriage plans amount to no more than his being attracted to a whore. Denouncing the mendacity of Georg's writing, the father asserts that not only does he know Georg's friend in Russia, but also that he has been in communication with him and therefore knows that this supposed friend "crumples Georg's letters unopened" while he holds up the father's letters to read them through.

For the reader in search of certainty the friend in Russia, a faraway reader himself, now may seem to be no more than a projection of the father's fantasy. The friend is, as the father says, the son that the father had always wanted. Perhaps this claim lies behind the way in which the friend is curiously related to the father's newspapers, for he is described as being "yellow enough to throw away". All that seems certain here is that the friend is a distant reader about whom the son can never know if he has received his communication or not. And Georg thus finds himself, like the reader, trying to decipher a situation as unknown as the father's newspaper, that enigmatic text described as "An old newspaper whose name was quite unknown to Georg"—"mit einem Georg schon ganz unbekannten Namen" (Raabe, 31). Georg can now only imagine his friend—and double—lost and ruined in the remote stretches of Russia, separated by the impossible distance any letter would have to traverse before, much as in "An Imperial Message," a revelation might come to him who awaits a message from a privileged space beyond.

For having written his "lying little letter," and perhaps for usurping the powers of the father (it is significant that Georg is implicitly accused of wanting sexual potency as much as for his writing: the pen and the penis belong to the father), Georg is condemned to death by drowning. It is an incongruous sentence that is as grotesque as the judge who is now portrayed as an old comedian, prancing on his bed. This parody of justice and interpretation sets forth another of Kafka's basic configurations. If the protagonist can be condemned, then one inevitably supposes that this condemnation is the manifestation of a law and that the judge knows and can communicate the law. But if there is a law, if there ever were a law, it is known only by a clown father who divulges no more than the sentence the supposed law imposes. The law exists only as an absence. Kafka's fiction seems to ask readers to suppose they are witnessing the workings of a law, of a superior order, perhaps of a logos; but the decreeing of the judgment does not, any more than the existence of the narrated text itself, guarantee the existence of a transcendent discourse. All that one can say with certainty is that in this story Georg, the would-be writer, stands condemned for his misrepresentations—and this condemnation effects an ironic metacommentary on the story itself. This final bit of implied self-reference leaves the reader caught in a hopeless interpretive circle.

A dutiful son, Georg carries out the sentence. He rushes to the bridge to throw himself into the water; and as he arrives he grasps the railings "as a starving man clutches at food." Georg has now replaced the father as the one who is in need of sustenance. This need, here as in other stories by Kafka, can result only in death, withdrawal, and silence. Georg's literal fall from the bridge at the end of "The Judgment" is at once a death and a fall into silence, and perhaps the fall of discourse finally into silence.

There is something comic, however, in the way that Georg's fall is a performance. The charwoman covers her face as he rushes by her on the steps. And he performs his self-execution, as the narrator says, with the skill of the gymnast that, to his parents' pride, he once was. This idealized image of the son as an athlete provides another ironic measure for his fall. Another Kafkan pattern emerges here: the hero falls from corporal self-sufficiency to hunger and then to death and silence, as in "A Hunger Artist" or, as in "The Metamorphosis," the next story I shall consider.

"The Judgment" and "The Metamorphosis"

In "The Metamorphosis" the protagonist's fall is perhaps more metaphorical than the fall in "The Judgment," since the hero does not
literally dive down to his death. Rather, as several generations of be-
mused or horrified readers have tried to imagine with some difficulty,
the main character, Gregor Samsa, awakens one morning and finds that
he has been transformed into a vermin, an *Ungeziefer* of human propor-
tions that may well stick in our mind as a big cockroach, especially
since the *Ungeziefer* is an image of pollution and defilement. I recall
that Karl Rossman was also treated as a vermin at the stoker's derisive
trial and that Kafka referred to himself as an *Ungeziefer* in his "Letter
to His Father" to stress that Kafka was convinced at times that this
image could best portray the fall from humanity into some state in
which one's very existence was a profanation of the law.

The fall into verminhood very quickly becomes a fall from the language that might explain the fall. This fall is also ironically measured
by the idealized image Gregor sees of himself when, scrambling to get
ready for work as he learns to use his new legs, he looks from the inner
space of his room, where he is isolated, into the outer family room or
the room of community space: "The breakfast dishes stood in great
number on the table, since for his father breakfast was the most important meal of the day, one he drew out for hours by reading various
newspapers. Straight across on the opposing wall hung a photograph of
Gregor, taken at the time of his military service, which showed how
he, as a lieutenant, with his hand on his dagger, smiling in a carefree
way, demanded respect for his carriage and his uniform" (modified
translation of pp. 100–101). This idealized image of Gregor is also associated with elements that Kafka had associated with discourse and
representation in "The Judgment." Gregor's father reads newspapers;
he is a consumer of texts as well as of the nourishment that his big
breakfast provides. In "The Metamorphosis" the father initially appears, like Georg's father, to be a weak figure—Gregor supports him
and the family—but he is also the inhabitant of the unproblematic
world where sustenance is available, in which the fallen discourse of
newspapers fills time, and in which sons with military bearing can command respect. The utter antithesis of this kind of son is the son who
exists as a profanation; and as such Gregor is excluded from the world
of sustenance and language and becomes a being who wonders if garbage will satisfy him.

Kafka's story begins one morning when Gregor, a hard-working traveling salesman, awakens to stare down at his wiggling legs and wonder

how he will get to work. Although he is a vermin who loses his capacity for language, he retains a human consciousness of his situation; and as in "The Judgment," much of the time the narrative point of view seems to espouse the character's perception. Kafka also broadens his narrative perspective at times to allow the reader to see Gregor as he is seen by those unfortunate enough to share his company. This strange and often comic dichotomy between Gregor's consciousness and his presence as a speechless vermin capable of making only "twittering squeaks" is heightened by the fact that neither Gregor nor his family ever ask how this metamorphosis could have occurred. It is as if he woke up with a very bad cold. Kafka is frustrating the doctor in every reader who wants to know the etiology of the sickness. Gregor is a monstrous presence that cries out for interpretation (which is a hyperbolic expression of Kafka's normal astonishment about the simple fact that things exist). Needless to say, interpretation has not been lacking.

In one perspective, for example, it seems true to say, as Wilhelm Emrich has put it, that Gregor "is interpretable only as the uninterpretable (*Uninterpretierbar*—which offers an appropriate Kafkan *Tier* or animal in the word itself).[10] Or, from another perspective, as Stanley Corngold has expressed it, "One sense of Gregor's opaque body is thus to maintain him as a solitude without speech or intelligible gesture, in the solitude of an indecipherable sign. To put it another way, his body is the speech in which the impossibility of ordinary language expresses its own despair."[11]

Kafka does, however, place interpreters of Gregor's actions within the story. His presence, acts, and intentions are interpreted, usually wrongly, by the story's characters, especially by the father. From this perspective it would appear that the characters again double the reader in hermeneutic inadequacy. The self-contained nature of "The Metamorphosis" also becomes clear when one sees, for example, that at the end of the first and the second part of the story the silent vermin is interpreted and judged by the father who, as an interpreter, stands as a comic double for the reader who attempts to decipher what Gregor's meaning might be. At the end of each of these parts the father's interpretations of Gregor's intentions result in violence that seems close to farce. In the first instance, when Gregor tries to return to his room, he has difficulty moving his new body, which lends itself to the worst of interpretations. And the judge-father gives the inexpert bug a good blow with a newspaper to drive him back into his own space. In the second instance the well-meaning beetle comes out of his room to try to help his sister, Grete, when his mother has fainted upon seeing her son. The father arrives in judgment again: "It was clear to Gregor that his father had taken the worst interpretation of Grete's all too brief statement and was assuming that Gregor had been guilty of some violent act" (120). The "worst interpretation" here results in the father's condemning Gregor, and so he bombards his scampering son with apples.

This strange judgment elicits the reader's interpretation. Apples recall the crime of original sin, but in this context I can hardly repress the feeling that Kafka is playing with Freudian notions about the relation of sons and fathers. The apples fly as if in some kind of farcical displacement of the castration fears that Freud ascribed to every son who would like to take the mother from the father. One should not, however, take Kafka's parodistic enactment of Freudian theory to mean that Kafka has written a Freudian allegory in which every event in Kafka's text illustrates some aspect of the way psychoanalytic theory describes the war between fathers and sons. On the contrary, Kafka's use of elements of Freudian theory—and this use seems quite self-conscious to me—is a way of disarming this interpretive tool before it can be applied.[12]

In the scene in which the father drives the son before him with a spray of round objects the parody destroys the genesis of meaning even as it invites the reader to use a Freudian as well as a biblical framework for interpretation. At the end of the episode it is clearly a Freudian moment for Gregor when he sees his mother fall, half undressed, into the father's arms. Gregor decides not to witness the primal scene that, according to Freud, haunts all children; and so upon viewing this sexually charged scene with the disrobed mother, the vermin son loses consciousness. The loss of consciousness is like a censure that cancels out the erotic scene—though of course what is erased is always present as in an absence that reminds us that it is still there.

The two violent scenes of paternal judgment join the fragmented presentation of the kind of Oedipal indices described by Freud and become part of the parody of hermeneutics that underlies most of Kafka's later works. Kafka's inscribing in his text references to the hermeneutic quest is his paradoxical if oblique way of making manifest that revelation is impossible. He is using paradoxical metalanguage with a vengeance; these statements about statements declare the incomprehensibility of the very statements that refer to themselves. This configuration appears again in the third and final part of "The Metamorphosis." In the third part Gregor completes his itinerary; he has gone from a self-sufficient body to a withering away in silence. He is condemned to disappear, to die, and to become the rubbish that the sturdy charwoman can discard. As in most of Kafka's stories, the object of interpretation—the text's central enigma as it were—is never brought to any elucidation. It merely effaces itself, like a hunger artist starving away, before the incommensurate problems it has posed. The story's task has been to trace this itinerary, to present the way in which the hermeneutic quest runs up against death and silence, against an entropic passage to final disorder.

A contrast to Gregor's demise is the final image of "The Metamorphosis." Gregor's sister, Grete, also undergoes a transformation, though one that opposes Gregor's. She awakens to her body's sufficiency once Gregor has disappeared. Standing in contrast to a vermin's need for the kind of sustenance that art or literature might offer is the self-contained sensuality of the sister's body as she stretches out in anticipation of the joys of marriage. Kafka concludes his story with an ending that asks no questions:

> [I]t struck both Mr. and Mrs. Samsa, almost at the same moment, as they became aware of their daughter's increasing vivacity, that in spite of all the sorrow of recent times, which had made her cheeks pale, she had bloomed into a pretty girl with a good figure. They grew quieter and half unconsciously exchanged glances of complete agreement, having come to the conclusion that it would soon be time to find a good husband for her. And it was like a confirmation of their new dreams and excellent intentions that at the end of their journey their daughter sprang to her feet first and stretched her young body. (139)

Grete has become an animal whose sensually awakened body needs no language to express its fulfillment. The symmetry with Gregor is converse, for he has become the animal whose condition cries out for language to mediate it; and this symmetry invests the entire story. Kafka opens "The Metamorphosis" with a declaration that Gregor's fall was "no dream" whereas Grete's accession to self-sufficient sexuality is part of the family's "new dreams." Perhaps this is Kafka's final irony: nightmares express fallen human reality better than do dreams of animal satisfactions.

Any single reading of "The Metamorphosis" will be inadequate, and readers must go back to the beginning and follow Gregor's itinerary again in order to grasp the play of self-reflexive interpretative mirrors that Kafka has placed along the way. On repeated readings, using the principle of the self-frustrating quest as their guide, readers can experience a coherence and an emotional tonality that escape their baffled first reading. If the interpretive quest underlies the general structure of "The Metamorphosis," the story owes its affective specificity to the way that Kafka uses particular objects, images, and situations to mirror the quest and to force the reader to enter a diffuse hermeneutic labyrinth.

The presence of objects in "The Metamorphosis" would appear to be dictated by the code of realistic narration that Kafka respects even as he narrates a fantastic event (but only *one* fantastic event). Kafka puts objects on his narrative stage that one would expect to find in the apartment of a traveling salesman who works hard, but hardly lives well. The descriptions of objects, as in Dickens or Flaubert, would at first seem to vouchsafe a certain stability and veracity to Kafka's fictional world, for this world seems to rest on the same premises that make up our presumably stable world.

Of course the first effect of Gregor's metamorphosis, in spite of the presence of an alarm clock telling him to get up, is that it subverts the realistic code, for the realistic mode that promises stability and hence readability is juxtaposed with totally gratuitous instability. But the code of realistic narration is never fully destroyed in the story. The code continues to ground the fantastic in what is a very ordinary or quotidian reality, in what is a most banally and thus sociologically average world. The radical incongruity between the fantastic and the banally real is, I think, another expression of that sense of the impossibility of bearing the real which is found in the "Conversation with the Supplicant"; the fantastic and the real are essentially two ways of looking at the same world, what one sees is a matter of perspective, though rarely does one see both the fantastic *and* the real so clearly. This incongruity springing from the opposition between fantastic metamorphosis and the code of realist narration forces the reader to scrutinize those objects that, in Flaubert, once promised to reveal the essence of the real. For they now seem contaminated by the fantastic.

In "The Metamorphosis," for example, how is the reader to make sense of a woman's picture in a room in which an ordinary man can awaken to find himself transformed into an insect? "Above the table upon which an unpacked sample collection of drapery was spread out—

Samsa was a traveling salesman—hung the picture that not long ago he had cut out of an illustrated magazine and had placed in a pretty, gilded frame. It showed a woman who, provided with a fur hat and a fur boa, sat upright and raised toward the viewer a thick fur muff in which her entire forearm had disappeared" (modified translation of p. 89). This strange, almost insulting image seems to acquire some meaning when, later, as Gregor's mother and sister begin to remove the furnishings from his room, Gregor tries to keep the picture in his room by pressing his vermin belly against it. The picture's own suggestive content plus the insect's comically sexual behavior obliges one to look for some kind of sexual theme here. Has Gregor's sexuality been projected onto or captured by some kind of fetishistic desire? Undoubtedly, but this reading—which one can hardly avoid—is short-circuited as soon as the reader realizes that the object on the wall is first of all an image, hence a form of representation, and as such, offers itself as another double for the story's representation of itself.

This way of reading the image through associations seems justified by the way that Kafka also associates the picture and its frame with newspapers, and newspapers are a recurrent emblem of a text's failure to have meaning or of inadequate language. The association occurs when, in the first part of the story, Gregor's mother explains to the irate chief clerk who has come to get Gregor for work how her dutiful son spends his time:

> The boy thinks about nothing but his work. It makes me almost cross the way he never goes out in the evenings; he's been here the last eight days and has stayed at home every single evening. He just sits there quietly at the table reading a newspaper or looking through railway timetables. The only amusement he gets is doing fretwork. For instance, he spent two or three evenings cutting out a little picture frame; you would be surprised to see how pretty it is; it's hanging in his room. . . . (95–96)

The chief clerk is indeed surprised when he views the room, though not for the same reasons as the reader who begins to grasp the way the textual elements tie together as self-referential signifiers.

Images can be associated with newpapers as forms of representation that fail to point beyond their status as doubles for the text itself. Newspapers in turn are associated with food, the sustenance that the story should give, but does not. After the metamorphosis Gregor's father apparently gives up reading newspapers aloud—perhaps a sign that he, too, is alienated from even this degraded form of logos?—and Gregor finds that his food is delivered to him on a newspaper by his sister after she finds that he no longer has a taste for the pure milk that he once liked:

> Gregor was wildly curious to know what she would bring instead, and made various speculations about it. Yet what she actually did next, in the goodness of her heart, he could never have guessed at. To find out what he liked she brought him a whole selection of food, all set out on an old newspaper. There were old, half-decayed veg-etables, bones from last night's supper covered with a white sauce that had thickened; some raisins and almonds; a piece of cheese that Gregor would have called uneatable two days ago. . . . (107–8)

Rotten cheese on a newspaper, this is the food that Gregor "sucked greedily at."

For the fallen vermin, for our everyman in search of some sustenance commensurate to his situation, garbage is the only nourishment that is appropriate. And if the reader feels that Kafka is parodying both the reader's desire for spiritual substance and the text's capacity to give him or her any such nourishment, the reader is not entirely wrong. Old newspapers covered with offal seem to be all that remains of the Word that once offered tastier repasts, an image that is at once derisive and plaintive in Kafka's world of comic anguish.

Not everyone is afflicted with such anguish, of course, such as the three lodgers whom the family takes in, briefly, in the third part of the story. They can eat great heaps of food before they turn to reading their newspapers: "They set themselves at the top end of the table where formerly Gregor and his father and mother had eaten their meals, un-folded their napkins, and took knife and fork in hand. At once his mother appeared in the other doorway with a dish of meat and close behind her his sister with a dish of potatoes piled high. The food steamed with a thick vapor" (128). The lodgers replace the family in a world where sustenance is a matter of course, where the vapor of a hearty meal seems to mask appearances, as does the smoke of their cigars when they turn to their newspaper: "The lodgers had already finished their supper, the one in the middle had brought out a news-paper and given the other two a page apiece, and now they were lean-ing back at ease reading and smoking" (129). The three with their full beards are related to those fathers in Kafka–fictional and real–for whom simple food is adequate and, by analogy, newspapers provide access to all that writing need reveal.

Kafka chooses precisely this moment when his three arrogant, self-complacent lodgers are ensconced in their chairs to make most clear the association between sustenance and art. Gregor's sister begins to play the violin. Having just said to himself (in vermin language, one supposes) that he is not hungry for the kind of food that the lodgers engorge with pleasure, Gregor is struck by the sound of music as if it were a call to some vestigial human part of himself. As Grete plays, Gregor comes out of his room: "Gregor crawled a little farther forward and lowered his head to the ground so that it might be possible for his eyes to meet hers. Was he an animal, that music had such an effect upon him? He felt as if the way were opening before him to the unknown nourishment he craved" (130–31). Kafka claimed to have no ear for music, which in a sense is all the more appropriate to this passage, for music is the promise of a sustenance that one cannot find, the promise of a revelation that does not occur as the notes unfold like so many foreshadowings of an annunciation. Gregor longs for a substance that nothing can grant him.

Objects—pictures, newspapers, food—function by representing within the text the inadequacy, if not the breakdown, of representation. This concern with representation also informs much of the way in which the Kafkan narrative unfolds; events, attitudes, suppositions in "The Metamorphosis" are largely grounded in misrepresentations. For example, after Gregor awakes at the story's beginning, he misrepresents his situation to himself. He struggles to get up and catch a train, wanting to believe that his newly acquired body is no more than a passing affliction, like a cold; and at the end of the story he still dreams at times of taking up his job again, of how with the next opening of the door he might "take the family's affairs in hand just as he used to do" (125). The reader also learns, after Gregor's awakening reflection on his situation, that he may have misrepresented his job security. As the head clerk storms about before Gregor's closed door, he yells that neither Gregor's security nor his reputation are as good as Gregor thinks. These are not Gregor's only delusions. It would appear that his family's situation, its capacity to get along without him and to fend for itself, has been misrepresented to Gregor. His father, it later appears, has some money set aside, and they are all capable of working diligently to make ends meet.

"The Judgment" and "The Metamorphosis"

These misrepresentations are revealed in various ways, but especially by metamorphoses, as we see when Gregor, who is about to be judged by his father at the end of the second part, looks up from his vermin's point of view and sees the man looming above him in his new uniform. This sickly father, who, Gregor thought, was not capable of getting up in the evening, is suddenly a transformed man, or, as Gregor notes in astonishment, this was not the father he had imagined to himself. "Now, however, he stood quite straight up, wearing a tight, blue uniform with gold buttons, such as attendants in banks wear. Over the high stiff collar of his coat flowed his strong double chin. From under his bushy eyebrows pierced forward sharply and attentively the stare of his dark eyes. His usually disheveled white hair was combed down and parted in a meticulous and precise glistening hair-style" (modified translation of p. 121).

Like Georg in "The Judgment," Gregor has been guilty of misrepresentations, and perhaps it is this implicit guilt that underlies the hero's fall and transforms Gregor's father, like Georg's, into a judge, into a being of strength who can now march on the once dominant son. There is no stability in this tale of metamorphosis, however; none of the representations or misrepresentations are certain, and in the third part of the story the father appears to have lost much of his power. He again undergoes a metamorphosis as he sleeps evenings in his uniform, soiling his coat, and becomes another victim of the *Dreck* that covers everything. (Recall his appearance at the story's "happy end.")

In the third part of the story, however, the key and exemplary misrepresentation turns primarily on the sister. As a prelude to his disappearance, Gregor indulges in a final fantasy representation when he wants to bring his sister into his room. Having hungered after the sustenance her violin playing promises, longing for a spiritual nourishment that this parasite without language cannot name, Gregor imagines how he might give affectionate solace to his sister after her playing is rejected by the three boarders. This fantasy of solace, whose incestuous overtones continue a parody of sexual thematics, finds its counterpart in Grete's final interpretation of the vermin. As she tells her mother and father: "You must just try to get rid of the idea that this is Gregor. The fact that we've believed it for so long is the root of all our trouble. But how can it be Gregor? If this were Gregor, he would have realized long ago that human beings can't live with such a creature. . ." (134). Grete's interpretation is both true and false. Kafka is wreaking havoc on the law of identity with the dialectic of misrepresentation. By applying throughout the story the kind of dream logic that allows one to be and not to be the same thing, to be Gregor and to be non-Gregor the vermin, Kafka creates the possibility for paradoxical misrepresentation at every level in "The Metamorphosis." And one may well see in this suspension of the law of identity, if one wishes, a characterization of our contemporary plight.

I address the question of dream logic and the rhetoric of dream in some detail in the fifth chapter of this study. In conclusion, in "The Metamorphosis" dream logic is at work in the creation of a realistic world in which the fantastic can happen without changing the basic order of that world. Dream logic suspends ordinary logic, and in this respect dream logic collaborates with self-referentiality in the creation of paradox. As with Grete's interpretation of Gregor, as with Gregor's interpretation of his father, every assertion made from a seemingly objective point of view readily finds a counterstatement within the fiction itself. This is a basic Kafkan pattern in the later stories and the unfinished novels, *The Trial* and *The Castle*. This pattern in which representation is revealed to be misrepresentation or contradiction grounds the Kafkan fiction in its own series of deforming mirror images. Meaning is generated not by reference to exterior discourses that the fictions use only in order to cancel them out; it is generated by a constant play of reference from one element in the story to another and back again. And as these elements—objects, events, attitudes and interpretations—show themselves to be forms of metalanguage that deny their own validity, the final effect is the creation of a self-annulling reference system that is a demonstration of the infinite and therefore null possibilities of hermeneutics.

"In the Penal Colony"

In 1913, the year after he completed "The Judgment" and "The Metamorphosis," Kafka's most notable achievement was writing some two hundred pages, as published, of letters to Felice Bauer, the woman Kafka had chosen for his fantasies about marriage. In 1914, however, Kafka had an extraordinarily productive period of writing fiction. He started work on *The Trial*, wrote the fragmentary "Nature Theater of Oklahoma" as a projected conclusion to *Amerika*, and wrote what many consider to be his most important short story, "In the Penal Colony." He was in no hurry to publish this story, and for a while he entertained the idea of publishing it with the two other stories in a single volume to be called *Strafen*—"Punishments." This project did not work out; and Kafka finally published "In the Penal Colony" in 1919, right before publishing the collection of short stories called *A Country Doctor*. Although World War I took place, with all its attendant hardships, in the years intervening between the story's writing and its publication, the war does not supply the context for interpretation that the story's publication date might suggest.

What the immediate interpretive context should be is difficult to put succinctly, since this "punishment" is a parable that takes the history of Western culture as its largest referential framework; and this history is meaningful only as a history of the writing of that history. It is only by understanding history—and perforce the writing thereof—that we might gain access to the law and logos that we once believed were at the origin of our history. To gain access to this story, however, I shall first limit my focus to the way that the story deals with the law and judgment and their relation to writing and discourse, and then turn to Kafka's view of history. "In the Penal Colony" spells out, as pun and literally, that the law and writing are two sides of the same thing—of that unnamable logos that we assume must exist. Writing is, in a quite literal sense, the means of finding access to the law, and hence to redemption, justification, and salvation. (*Erlösung* is the received term for salvation that Kafka uses, derisively, in the story itself.) In this exemplary story, then, the equation between writing and the law is savagely clear: writing is a way of finding the law as well as the form of the law itself.

The identification of writing with the law is given literal expression by the story's writing and punishing machine. This machine is far more than a simple torture device that seems to foreshadow our science fiction dreams of what one might achieve with the proper application of cybernetics. It is a machine that writes the law, or if one prefers, inscribes revelation in the flesh. In the story's bizarre prison colony there is no need for trials, or even for the condemned to be told their crime, because the writing machine grants the condemned a revelation of the law when it writes the law on the body of the prisoner who is strapped in the machine. By granting access to the law through this inscription, by making the word flesh as it were, the machine should bring about the promised redemption that the story's protagonist, the explorer, looks for, but does not find when the machine's guardian immolates himself on it.

A brief résumé of the story will help to orient my discussion. It is noteworthy that this story has a sufficiently traditional type of plot that is amenable to a résumé. As the title suggests, "In the Penal Colony" is set in a colony where, until recently, it seems punishment has been the principal occupation. An explorer comes to the island where the colony is located and is asked to witness an execution on the contraption that writes the sentence—in a twelve hour ordeal—on the condemned prisoner's body. This practice, he learns, is probably about to be abolished by the colony's new commandant. The machine's keeper tells the explorer that the executions were once celebrated by multitudes who thronged to witness them in festive rapture. At this execution, however, the explorer finds himself virtually alone, with the machine's guardian, a soldier, and the condemned prisoner. The guardian suddenly entreats the explorer to help him in his scheme to preserve the machine. When the explorer refuses to go along with him, the guardian, in an unexpected move, releases the prisoner and gets on the machine himself; he programs it to write on him with its sharp needles the rather vacuous commandment "BE JUST." The machine breaks down, however, and begins to spew forth its innards, and rather than write on the guardian, it impales him with a spike through the forehead. Indeed, this self-murder hardly looks like the expected redemption.

In what is a brief epilogue the explorer then returns to the island's town, where, in a tea room, he comes across the old commandant's gravestone set under a table. This kind of expressionist distortion points to how much Kafka is part of that era that produced artists like Nolde, Beckmann, and Kokoschka; and expressionistic is the only way to characterize the weird religious parable that seems to be unfolding here. For, before the explorer leaves, forcing the prisoner and the soldier to remain behind him on the island, he learns that according to a prophecy the old commandant will rise again and lead his adherents to "recover the colony." Apparently, the civilized modernity of the new commandant will be abolished by the return of true believers.

"In the Penal Colony" is narrated directly and indirectly through the consciousness of the explorer, as the English translation calls him. In German, however, he is *der Reisende*, literally the traveler, a term that can also designate a commercial traveler such as Gregor Samsa. The explorer is one of Kafka's voyagers, on his way from one point to another, though Kafka indicates no precise space for this travel. The penal colony itself is a point on a trajectory that is, moreover, as much temporal as spacial: the *Reisende* is making a trip back in time as well as through space. At first the traveler appears to be something of a foil character, eliciting a description of the barbarous machine that now appears on the point of being abolished. Endowed with a Western and liberal sense of civilization and its requirements, he has come to the colony and has been asked to observe a barbarous ritual so that his evidence and reproval can be used in abolishing the practice. All of this is largely hypothetical because it is the machine's guardian who supplies the reader with various conjectures as to why the explorer is there at all.

Narrative point of view only infrequently coincides directly with the explorer's consciousness. Kafka uses this direct coincidence selectively when, for example, the narrator reflects that the explorer is not afraid to refuse to help the guardian. Or when, curiously enough, the explorer understands that the guardian should want to immolate himself on the machine out of the strength of his convictions. But much of the time the traveler reflects a kind of neutral observer's point of view. And what he feels about what he sees and hears is approximately what any enlightened European, such as the reader, would feel in such strange circumstances.

What Kafka has achieved with this varying narrative perspective can be likened to what might be the result of sending a television reporter into a time warp; he finds that tradition has been preserved, for the moment, in this marginal colony situated remotely on the fringes of our civilization (and I invite the reader to think about analogous centers of marginality in his or her own culture). Thus it would be an error to see prefigured in the colony some prophetic political commentary. Rather, I think that Kafka is concerned with the way access to the law and the Word were once perceived to be literally connected with a kind of material self-evidence that we can hardly understand today. This is one meaning of the belief that the Messiah makes the Word into flesh. Perhaps more apposite is the example of Dante's Inferno where the truth of judgment, the justice of the law, is inscribed in the bodies of the condemned in the form of the totally appropriate punishment that the divine logos has decreed to be their lot. But the visionary truth of Dante's cosmology is reduced today to the kinds of marginal fanaticisms that reflect nonetheless what once was the truth and which somehow we continue to live by even beyond the advent of our modernity. The explorer has entered a time warp where the victim of the law as it once was and a tattered vision of the law as it is are preserved simultaneously.

A German proverb holds that he who does not obey must feel, and Kafka's rather literal application of this lesson points to the derisive, almost "camp" side of the enactment of punishment as ritual murder. One may have to remind oneself at times that Kafka is a comic genius. It is, however, this comic sense that is at work forcing us to interpret the story at once in terms of the most banal proverbs and the great monuments of our cultural history, in terms of the Bible or at least the biblical overtones found throughout the story. The machine is set in a "sandy valley, a deep hollow surrounded on all sides by naked crags." A number of biblical valleys immediately suggest themselves as possible references here, such as the valley of tears; or Gehenna, the Jewish version of Hell, or the valley of Joel 4, the valley of the last judgment. And the Christian may find some oblique reference to the valley that was the scene of Christ's passion. All of these references work, at least to the extent that they point to the kind of world in which it made sense to speak of the union of the flesh and the word, and they are utterly dysfunctional to the extent that the biblical text speaks of a world that no longer exists for modern man.

Other derisive aspects of this black comedy turn on the condemned himself, who, like all of us, is ignorant of the law. Like all who ignore the law, those dogs and vermin that populate Kafka's bestiary, the condemned prisoner is a grotesque animal. He is like a "submissive dog that one might have thought he could be left to run free on the surrounding hills and would only need to be whistled for when the execution was due to begin" (140). The prisoner who is to receive the revelation of the word is actually something of a cannibal, for he was condemned as much for having threatened to "eat" his superior as for the crime of falling asleep while on watch. A savage beast, a cringing dog, such is the victim of what one might take for a mock passion.

The machine itself is described with a precision that comically contrasts with the way it flies apart once it is finally set in motion. Kafka creates a grotesque farce as he describes the preparations necessary for being mutilated on the machine. The guardian is short of parts for his machine; he has not, for example, replaced the felt bit that the condemned man places in his mouth. The bit is so filthy that it causes the prisoner to vomit all over the machine when the stinking felt is placed in his mouth. This is farce based on pure gesture and incongruity, and Kafka uses it throughout the story. When the machine breaks down, it throws parts out in a display of its infinite capacity to generate cogs and wheels—much like those silent film comedies in which machines demonstrate their humanlike capacity to go berserk.

But the machine also has a near sacerdotal function for the true believer. That true believer is the guardian who, like a priest explaining a rite to a nonbeliever, gives the explorer an account of the machine's history and its function. The guardian—who is also called an officer in the story—is an anachronism, at least from a modern European's point of view. He has dedicated himself to the preservation of tradition in our post-Enlightenment era, and with the tradition of the writing machine, to the preservation of the written law. For he is also a judge. In a Kafkan perspective judges are by definition those who should know the law and the sacred principles that they apply, and for once this is the case. Or as the guardian explains: "'This is how the matter stands. I have been appointed judge in this penal colony. Despite my youth. For I was the former Commandant's assistant in all penal matters and know more about the apparatus than anyone. My guiding principle is this: Guilt is never to be doubted'" (145).

This judge is armed with the certainty of a principle that appears to have a kind of a priori certainty about it, for who can ever say that he or she has not broken the law, especially when it is never really clear (except perhaps to the judge) what the law is? This principle allows the judge-guardian to proceed with machinelike efficiency in the (literal) application of the law to the hides of the accused so that they discover what their guilt is in the moment of revelation.

Kafka's basic premise is that we never have a revelation of the law before the judgment; or, alternately, that we only deduce from the judgment that there must be a law. Perhaps I might best elaborate this essential point by a brief comparison with his parable "Before the Law." This parable appears in the novel *The Trial*, though Kafka removed it from that framework when, as I noted earlier, he published it as a separate text in *A Country Doctor*. In the context of *The Trial* the parable is told by a priest who seeks to explain to Joseph K. the nature of the "trial" he must undergo after he has been arrested, although no charges have been brought forward. Kafka obviously thought this parable about the inaccessibility of the law, of some justifying logos, could stand alone to illustrate how we continue to believe in the necessity of some higher principles even when we are refused any certain knowledge of them. In the parable a man from the country spends his life before the gate that should give him access to the law, but the gate's guardian never allows him to enter—even if, as the man learns as he dies, the entrance was meant only for him. One asks why did the guardian not grant access to the man from the country?

This question brings up, in turn, other questions as it engages the readers in hermeneutic questions about the parable and a "proper" interpretation of its enigma. A semantic labyrinth takes shape to which we readers would like to have access. For it seems the parable itself is as obscure as the unknown law that the man seeks. If this is the case, then perhaps the parable is a double for the law that it would represent. The text would then be a double for its own meaning, which again brings up the paradoxes of self-referential language that I discussed earlier. The parable represents itself as access to the meaning of the parable, and hence to writing, and consequently to writing as the law. But how can one know the meaning of the parable unless one already knows the law—and vice versa. All writing is caught up in this circularity as in a maze that demands interpretations that generate other interpretive parables—as occurs in fact in *The Trial*—that once again demonstrate the null possibilities of hermeneutics.

By contrast, the guardian of the penal colony's machine has no such difficulties in that he has a principle upon which to base his practice as a judge, or so he *believes*. Belief is the essence of his certainty, for he offers nothing else upon which to base his principle. Certainly his belief hardly seems congruent with the grotesque image of the machine going haywire while he is committing suicide. But the guardian believes that he is a protector of the truth and the law, and a good part of the narration turns on his attempt to persuade the traveler to go along with his scheme to defend the judicial practices against the new commandant. He claims to preserve the memory of a period when justice was a public event, when the law could be made manifest to the crowds who would gather in the valley to see the judgment; when, as he says, children were encouraged to observe the edifying lesson:

> It was impossible to grant all the requests to be allowed to watch it from nearby. The Commandant in his wisdom ordained that the children should have the preference; I, of course, because of my office had the privilege of always being at hand; often enough I would be squatting there with a small child in either arm. How we all absorbed the look of transfiguration [*Verklärung*] on the face of the sufferer, how we bathed our cheeks in the radiance of that justice, achieved at last and fading so quickly! (154)

Kafka is a sharp critic of the deceitfulness of memory, for memory can claim to justify anything precisely because there are few criteria for checking the claims of memory. The guardian can presumably remember transfigurations brought about by the revelation of the law as it was written out, as it manifested itself as writing. But what can justify that memory when nothing on the island or in the barren valley speaks to the guardian's claim?

The guardian wishes to adduce other evidence to support his claims. He has writings about the machine in the form of the first commandant's plans for the machine. These plans are a possible guide for interpreting the machine and its writings, what I would call a potential guide for hermeneutics. The guardian insists that the explorer look at these plans so that he, too, can appreciate the machine's design and the commandant's intent. The explorer, our representative of enlightened consciousness, looks at these plans with much interest, but he only sees "a labyrinth-like series of repeatedly crossing lines that covered the paper so densely that only with great effort could one make out the white interstices" (and, unlike the available translation, the German original makes clear that writing is a labyrinth: he sees "labyrinthartige, einander vielfach kreuzende Linien, die so dicht das Papier bedeckten, dass man nur mit Mühe die weissen Zwischenräume erkannte" (R, 107). This guide for the perplexed is another one of Kafka's images of the maze that is a double for writing and, by implication, the law. The guardian urges the explorer to read the plans, but all the European traveler can recognize is their "artistic quality"— "Es ist sehr kunstvoll," he says, "It is very artful," but he cannot decipher the plans.

This rather droll image of the explorer yielding to the enthusiast's urging presents one of Kafka's most effective portrayals of writing, reading, and interpretation. Peering at an artful, but dense series of scratchings, the explorer is asked to undertake exegesis, to understand in this Kafkan metacommentary how a set of incomprehensible plans can explain an insane, dysfunctional killing machine.

The labyrinth that the explorer faces is not quite like the one that Karl Rossman confronts in *Amerika* when he finds himself wandering in the corridors below deck or when, later, he tries to negotiate the nocturnal hallways of the country house that, in disobeying his uncle, he goes to. *Amerika's* mazes are spacial configurations, whereas the explorer's labyrinth is the one created by the need to interpret cultural practices—beliefs and customs—that an outsider cannot understand so long as he stands outside the wall that these practices draw about themselves. Kafka's traveler is an explorer in the sense that he must enter into a cultural maze from which he is excluded by his Enlightenment skepticism. The guardian's suicidal gesture might then be seen as the desperate attempt to communicate to the traveler the full measure of his belief. When he finally sees that the explorer will not help him in his rather incoherent scheme, he releases the prisoner and demands that the explorer read the papers telling how the machine operates. This time the guardian spells out the brief text, "BE JUST," that he says he is going to insert in the machine. But the explorer still fails to decipher what is written out. He can only reply that he, too, is prepared to believe that the text is there, written out as the officer claims it is.

Kafka's irony merits close attention here. Is the explorer being taken into the labyrinth of belief here? He does say that he "understands" the guardian's killing himself. And if this comprehension is authentic, is it a double for the kind of comprehension that readers may feel, which would be Kafka's ironic way of demonstrating that we can all be drawn into the true believer's need for the law? I would even claim that this is Kafka's most pointed demonstration of our cultural schizophrenia, a state in which we are all at once divided within ourselves into believers needing the law and skeptics dubious about our deepest needs.

If readers are not willing to go so far as I propose in seeing a potential fanatic in themselves, readers must nonetheless enter the hermeneutic maze and ask why has the officer, preparing to immolate himself, prepared his little imperative as the law he wants revealed to himself by his beloved machine? What "transfiguration" does he seek by writing this imperative on his body?

If we take the guardian's first principle at its word, then we must grant of course that he, like everyone, is guilty. If that seems clear enough, then it would appear that he perforce has violated the commandment "BE JUST." This commandment is the most general of all principles, for it is the precondition for obedience to all laws. In that its generality is a necessary condition one might also say that this principle is the emptiest of commandments, though one that has most certainly been violated if we are all guilty.

There is an extremely derisive side to the guardian's immolating himself for a principle that has all the force of "Be Good" or "Obey the Law," especially when we cannot know the law in the first place. In this sense the principle is vacuous to the second degree. And the demonstration of this vacuum is completed when the officer kills himself on the machine. The machine merely reveals that it is no longer a machine for revelation, for the law does not manifest itself as writing. It reveals itself as a mangling in one last bloody murder. An empty law, a broken-down machine for murderous epiphanies, this is apparently what the past has bequeathed us, or at least our prison colonies.

"In the Penal Colony" opens up onto the past and a concern with history in a more explicit way than do most of the earlier short stories, though, as in "Investigations of a Dog," history is a central theme in some of the texts of the *Nachlass*. In the most general terms, Kafka's views of history are presupposed by his views about the inaccessibility of the law and the fall of language. In this respect Kafka's view of history—in both the intertwining senses of an event and the recording in writing of the event—is the necessary backdrop for understanding most of Kafka's writings. History is the simple passage of time that produces the fall away from a time when there might have been a coincidence between the law and language and mankind might have known a divine logos uniting the two as the will of the Father.

Paradoxically, as Kafka's narrator claims in "Investigations of a Dog," it was knowledge that took men and dogs down the road that led away from that moment in the past when we had certain knowledge. History is also a form of knowledge as well as the temporal process of which we must have knowledge if we are to understand why we have no (true) knowledge. Hegel may have been the first to show that all history must necessarily be knowledge about the mind that writes the history of that mind, but Kafka shows the paradoxical side of this self-referential state of affairs that finally reduces history to a mere set of claims about itself.

Kafka's dog researcher questions whether history is a form of progress; and in whatever sense we understand history, this hardly seems to be the case. The great increase in scientific knowledge in dogdom has merely led to a fall, or as our dog savant puts it:

> No, whatever objection I may have to my age, former generations were not better, indeed in a sense they were far worse, far weaker. Even in those days wonders did not openly walk the streets for anyone to seize; but all the same, dogs—I cannot put it in any other way—had not yet become so doggish as today, the edifice of dogdom was still loosely put together, the true Word could still have intervened, planning or replanning the structure, changing it at will, transforming it into its opposite; and the Word was there, was very near at least, on the tip of everybody's tongue, anyone might have hit upon it. And what has become of it today? (299–300)

Analogies are plentiful between the tale of dogdom and "In the Penal Colony." The guardian, like one of the dogs of time gone by, still has the Word, or at least the old commandant's plans for the writing machine. Moreover, he still has memories of the wonders, the *Wunder*, or miracles that have disappeared from history. He remembers the miraculous transfigurations wrought by the revelation of the True Word. As a true believer he can remember what the dog researcher says has disappeared from history.

Kafka's allegories about the nature of history can apply to a number of views of history, though of course the first view that comes to mind is the one that has underwritten much of our history: the biblical version of the initiation of history as man's coming to knowledge and thus undergoing a fall. This fall is not only a past event, but it continues, for Kafka and for theologians, as a recurring structure of the present. Or, as Kafka put it in one of the posthumously published notebooks when he mused on the nature of paradise: "The expulsion from Paradise is in its main significance eternal: Consequently the expulsion from Paradise is final, and life in this world irrevocable, but the eternal nature of the occurrence (or, temporally expressed, the eternal recapitulation of the occurrence) makes it nevertheless possible that not only could we live continuously in Paradise, but that we are continuously there in actual fact, no matter whether we know it here or not."[13] Kafka's logic is impeccable, for if we are constantly undergoing a fall, we must perpetually be in paradise. The paradox of perpetually falling is that we always are living through the past's fall as a repetition, a *Wiederholung,* in the present. In this meditation, taken from a *Notebook,* Kafka does not see our fall as being due to knowledge, but rather to the fact that "we have not yet eaten of the Tree of Life." What the Tree of Life might be is not entirely clear, though I suspect that it must be viewed in the biblical context as having some relation with the true Word. In any case, these few reflections show that Kafka, when not writing allegory, also conceived of the fall as an ongoing process, to be measured in each present moment by the loss of the paradise in which we are powerless to remain. In the case of "In the Penal Colony" the fall is embodied in the decadence that has led from the crowd's jubilation to the barren days of the story's present moment, all of which can be contained within the memory span of one man, the guardian-judge; for in this character Kafka mockingly portrays the fall, in the present, from belief to mangling.

I stress the importance of memory again, since Kafka suggests that the fall that constitutes the essential nature of history can be grasped by memory. One wonders if this fall is not in a sense created by memory. In many short pieces Kafka's reference to memory seems to underscore that memory is responsible for our notions of history and our belief in a fall. For example, in the unfinished parable "The Animal in the Synagogue" a strange beast inhabits the temple. At first the story suggests that the pale blue-green animal, the size of a marten, is some temporary intruder that has accidentally wandered into the religious edifice. The building itself seems to be already suffering from the passage of time: "If only one could communicate with the animal, one could, of course, comfort it by telling it that the congregation in this little town of ours in the mountains is becoming smaller every year and that it is already having trouble in raising the money for the upkeep of the synagogue. It is not impossible that before long the synagogue will have become a granary or something of the sort and the animal will then have the peace it now so sorely lacks" (*PP,* 51). The animal is obliquely associated with a fall, the fall of the synagogue, perhaps of the covenant itself, as the narrator reports it, and this fall in turn is a metonymy for the fall from the true Word.

As this parable progresses, however, the temporal framework goes askew. The animal that at the story's outset is described as a *temporary* disturbance is then described as having been present for years. With this new temporal perspective the narrator says that the little beast is terrified by the divine service, and wonders why the animal has not become accustomed to it; he wonders if this anguish is due to a memory of times long past or a premonition of future times. The temporal framework finally turns in upon itself, so to speak; it veers into the past as the narration changes tenses. This shift in tenses is consonant with the view of history that sees the past as a structure repeating itself in the present (the present as always having already existed). And suddenly it seems that there has always been, as far as memory allows recall, an animal in the synagogue:

> Many years ago, so it is recounted, attempts were really made to drive the animal away. It is possible, of course, that this is true, but it is more likely that such stories are mere inventions. There is evidence, however, that at that time the question whether the presence of such an animal might be tolerated in the house of God was investigated from the point of view of the Law and the Commandments. Opinions were sought from various celebrated rabbis, views were divided. . . . (*PP*, 57)

The animal has become a historical institution, eliciting legal opinions and opening the door to the hermeneutic maze. The parable has moved from the memory of the possible profanation of the temple to the institutionalization of the animal as part of the synagogue's "history." From memory the move is to stories, myths, inventions, interpretations, all turning on the interpretation of the law; finally the memories about the animal become part of the communal history that underwrites the covenant itself—and it is the Ark of the Covenant that seems to attract the little beast.

Memory generates the repetition that becomes codified and elaborated in histories if not history. If Kafka could not finish this wonderful parable, perhaps it was because he could not let himself be seduced by the idea of a closure that would eliminate his beast, or force the reader to assign some meaning to it that might put an end to the range of meaning the animal can have. In spite of what the narrator says, it is difficult to believe that the narrator's grandfather is ever going to climb up and catch it. There is no possible closure for writing that is based on the view of history as eternal repetition, and like the animal's anguish, the eternal repetition concerns past memories as much as future premonitions.

The guardian of the machine has his memory, and in the perspective of "In the Penal Colony" memory is the force that generates fidelity to the legends and myths to which the enlightened have no access. For modern man access to the law is through writing, since we judge that writing is the necessary condition for the existence of history (if there are no written texts, there can only be the archaeological research that attempts to make speak the mute records that cultures without writing leave behind). Writing is the recording of memory, and in Kafka's work this writing is also a form of fall. The fall into writing is another version of the fall that all history entails, hence the inevitable decadence of texts, the disintegration of books, for their writing *is* history.

Two other key texts, both written in 1917, "The New Advocate" and "An Old Manuscript," further illustrate this theme of history and writing. The first story describes the reception of a new lawyer, Dr. Bucephalus, who was once the horse of Alexander the Great. Given this horse's important role in "world history," today he must be granted special consideration, or at least a friendly reception. For, as the narrator puts it, there is no longer an Alexander the Great, even if there are still plenty of those who know how to murder people over a banqueting table. Today, in the decadent present, no one "can blaze a trail to India" (415). The *distance* is too great to be crossed, and "the gates have receded to remoter and loftier places." This expansion of space is, in Kafka's work, a correlate to the fall into time, for both space and time are measures of the distance that separates the fall from the true Word and thus the impossibility of messages ever arriving from the origins of the law. Given this expansion of space, then, Bucephalus, the animal lawyer, does what is best for all fallen animals looking for some trace of the past, which is to "absorb oneself in law books," and to turn the pages of ancient tomes in which writing apparently could be a compensation for the fall that the writing is witness to.

Books come apart, however, and often the violence of history remains only as "Ein altes Blatt"—an old sheet of paper (translated as "An Old Manuscript"). This little parable shows there truly are many who rage and kill, for the text describes in the present tense the occupation of the emperor's capital by ravenous nomads who speak no recognizable language. They express their elementary needs by screams and by tearing great hunks of flesh from living animals. Outside of writing, outside of language in any form, these nomads are violence personified in the destruction of the present moment. Readers encounter this savagery, however, in an "old sheet," a detached piece of paper from some lost manuscript or destroyed parchment, and thus they know that these acts of rapine and plundering are part of the past. These acts constitute a past that exists in writing as a present, as a repetition in the present of the past's fall as violence and destruction. And so the page narrates that the emperor withdraws, as he has always withdrawn, as he will always be withdrawn in Kafka's abolition of tenses, leaving salvation to "us artisans and tradesmen" whose memories generate the perpetual text of the fall (417).

To recapitulate and elaborate upon these historical themes, or themes of history, as they appear in the story "In the Penal Colony," let me turn again to the story's location. The island location of the prison colony with its cruel judicial practices is seemingly remote from present Western civilization. The reader may first take the colony's machine as something of a relic, left over from some historical period that has preceded our presumably more progressive era. The machine perhaps once had some justification; the guardian claims it once produced revelation and transfiguration in accord with the old commandant's now incomprehensible plans. But all that speaks to such a claim is the tale told by a judge who relies on his memory to describe a once glorious past. His belief in the past is so strong that he garners some sympathy and distant comprehension from the explorer when he chooses to die on the machine rather than deny the machine and all that it stands for. In this sense the guardian is a martyr to the writing-torture machine, and, with rather savage irony, this desire for self-immolation points to the relation that the seeker of the law, or the interpreter of texts, has with the object of his labors.

Specifically with regard to history, it is evident that if, as the officer would have it, the writing machine were ever a source of ecstatic revelation, it was in a past that is now beyond recall (for the last man to remember it is now a part of that legendary past). Finally, all the present offers is a display of writing's dysfunctionality, though with great comic gusto. The machine's explosive exhibition of its innards is the kind of parody of the fall of writing that Harpo Marx might have illustrated.

This parody is continued, if not completed, when the traveler finds the former commandant's tomb; it lies incongruously under a table in a tea house where its gravestone promises that the commandant will return and recover the colony. This is a farcical distortion of the Christ or Messiah myth, though of course it can be taken to refer to any resurrection myth that promises some form of redemption occurring in history:

> They pushed one of the tables aside, and under it there was really a gravestone. It was a simple stone, low enough to be covered by a table. There was an inscription on it in very small letters, the explorer had to kneel down to read it. This was what it said: "Here rests the old Commandant. His adherents, who now must be nameless, have dug this grave and set up this stone. There is a prophecy that after a certain number of years the Commandant will rise again and lead his adherents from this house to recover the colony. Have faith and wait!" (167)

Engraved on the stone is the final image of writing, in a prophetic mode that promises some intervention of the father figure in the course of history. Writing inscribed in stone aims at the future, whereas meaningful writing inscribed in flesh seems to have been possible only in the past. The two types of writing are joined, however, in their being inscribed in a history that repeats the fall in such a way that past and future are always already here.

In theological terms this looks like a nearly satirical allegory about revelation and eschatology, or perhaps, in equally Jewish terms, of the relation of the people to the promise of the Covenant. But I would stress that Kafka is offering us an open allegory aiming at the multiple ways we wish to make sense of history, and one would not be going far amiss here to see a mocking view of the triumph of history such as that which Marxism once proposed in its more militant days. The reader must entertain symbols that, in their inadequacy to explain history (or anything else), are annulled with the same gesture that the writing machine directs at the guardian. The story makes an allusion to Christ or to some messiah-like figure in order to show that the joining of word to flesh is only as functional or dysfunctional as the writing machine for which the avenging messiah would be a double. The Christ symbol is *present*, but mainly as a demonstration of how the historical Word has fallen into a derisive discourse that mocks its own inadequacy.

Kafka's irony does not stop with this demonstration, for the spectators in the tea house are aware that the Word inscribed in stone, the old commandant's prophecy, is deserving of ridicule—and yet the explorer does not mock this extravagant claim. Rather, he leaves in haste. Kafka thus closes off the narrative perspective at the end of the story so that the readers do not see from within how the traveler reacts to this final example of writing. Kafka is content to describe how the explorer uses rope to drive back the prisoner and the soldier so that they cannot accompany him on the boat on which he continues his journey. But the reader cannot help wondering why the explorer turns on his heels at the sight of the stone.

Does the explorer finally find himself, in spite of himself, caught up in the promise of writing? There is something curiously biblical in the image of his driving off the poor with a rope, perhaps by its association with Christ and the money changers in the temple—though the import is totally reversed. In any case, the story's conclusion curiously undermines the undermining that the story has proposed until the explorer's departure at the end. It suggests that the Enlightenment mind is not always capable of dealing easily with those structures of meaning that, ironically enough, we, like Marx, have consigned to the ashcans of history.

I shall conclude these considerations of "In the Penal Colony" by recalling that Kafka returned once more to the messiah myth, in quite explicit terms, in a later story published in *A Country Doctor,* "Jackals and Arabs." This tale's narrator is another traveling European who is visiting an exotic civilization. While traveling in the desert, he camps one night in an oasis. Here a band of jackals approach him, seize him, and inform him that he is the one that their ancestors had foretold. He is to bring cleanliness to them by taking a pair of shears and cutting the Arabs' throats. As the jackals offer him a pair of rusty sewing scissors, a laughing Arab arrives, tells the European that the jackals tell their tale to every traveler, and then the Arab drives them back with a typical Kafkan whip. As if to show the traveler the true nature of the jackals, the Arab has thrown to them a camel carcass that the beasts fall upon in fury. Truly fallen beasts, these meat eaters nonetheless have their myths that tie them to origins and promise them a future when the word will come and with it, the purification of their filth-loving nature. The jackals are not unlike the true believers of the prison colony, though their situation can be even more easily likened to that of the Jews, Christians, or any people or sect that live awaiting the realization of their prophetic texts. Yet the jackals' desires are contradictory, for their behavior belies their desire for cleanliness. In this way their decadence becomes a part of their myth that would promise their redemption. The fall is thus necessary for salvation, for only with the fall can the jackals have their myths of redemption. Perhaps we can understand the flight of the traveler in Kafka's "In the Penal Colony" in this light. With the demise of the true believer, with the fall of the fall, there is no longer either fall or promise of redemption. There is only the world of the ongoing tedium of our modernity.

A Country Doctor

In the letter Kafka left on his desk requesting the destruction of his work he declared that he was satisfied with little of what he had written. He named approvingly "The Judgment," "The Metamorphosis," "The Stoker," "In the Penal Colony," "The Hunger Artist," and *A Country Doctor*.[14] In this list only *A Country Doctor* is a collection of short stories, which suggests that in this work Kafka felt he had achieved something he had not accomplished elsewhere. This impression is confirmed when one notes that Kafka also expressed his hesitant approbation of *A Country Doctor* in his diaries. I quote an entry from 25 September 1917: "I can still have passing satisfaction from works like *A Country Doctor*, provided I can still write such things at all (very improbable). But happiness only if I can raise the world into the pure, the true, and the immutable." Kafka's goals have been realized only approximately, if at all, in these stories—by his own standards, that is. For this diary entry also makes clear that Kafka made the impossible demand of art that it reveal some pure metaphysical truth. In asking for "the pure, the true, and the immutable" Kafka yearns for a metaphysical revelation the possibility of which his fiction constantly places in doubt. Kafka had good reason to be happy with *A Country Doctor*, but more for the way in which he undermines a belief in metaphysics, for Kafka's actual accomplishments in this collection are the very opposite of his wish to offer metaphysical purity which, as Kafka also speculated, would destroy literature in a burst of apocalyptic certainty.

I think the first major claim one can make for Kafka is that in a number of stories of this collection he mastered his own form of expressionist dream rhetoric for the narration of fiction. The creation of narrative strategies and techniques based on the rhetoric of dream was, in Kafka's mind, part of a search for the revelation of essential truths. As he told his young friend Gustav Janouch, dream unveils the reality behind which the idea (*Vorstellung*) remains. It is noteworthy that Kafka then adds that this is the terrifying side of life and the side of art that shakes us. Dream does not, apparently, reveal the immutable truth of Platonic metaphysics (which Max Brod wanted to find in Kafka's work), but the *Schreckliche*—a terrifying truth.[15] Kafka thus speaks at once of his desire to find essential revelation through dreams and the way that dreams shake us with what I perceive as the failure of revelation.

Before making a few general comments on Kafka's creation of a dream rhetoric, I shall illustrate concretely what I mean by a story based on dream. In the preceding chapter I discussed this collection's first story, "The New Advocate," in connection with Kafka's view of history. But this tale is also amenable to a reading as a dream text. It can be read as the horse-centered narration of a dream in which the narration juxtaposes impossible events occurring in an implausible world in which time no longer obeys normal laws. The horse of Alexander the Great has survived and in our time of decadence has decided that the only solution for him is to become a lawyer. A reading of the story based upon the rhetoric of allegory will of course offer one interpretation of Dr. Bucephalus; it will find abstract ideas or a symbolic drama enacted here as a parable. And this procedure allows for ironic interpretations that are necessary for reading this text within the context of the fall of law into history. But at the same time the fantastic temporal span is a suspension of the laws governing normal reality; and we know that the one realm in our daily experience (other than animated cartoons) wherein horses can talk or study law books without concern for time is dream. I would not claim that Kafka narrates a dream in the sense that he has merely described what he or someone else might once have dreamed at night; rather, I would propose that in this story he has drawn upon the narrative techniques that preside over the elaboration of dream. The dream suspension of the "laws" of normal reality is analogous to the suspension of law that history inevitably seems to bring about—and I refer to all senses of law as a code for events and behavior, as a secure guide and a logos.

In this exploration of what dream can offer the artist or the thinker Kafka is part of a literary and scientific movement that—from the Romantics through Freud, Jung, and the surrealists—has attempted to explore dream as a form of discourse; or, conversely, has attempted to see what the rhetoric of dream can offer for the creation of new discourses. In the case of Kafka this exploration of dream led to the creation of parables about waking reality's *peu de réalité*, its sparseness of reality, as the surrealist André Breton put it.

Clearly one of the most intriguing aspects of dream narration is that it can unfold while paying no attention to the laws of logic. Dream can suspend the logical law of identity, the law of the excluded middle, and the requirements of noncontradiction. One can be and not be at the same time in a dream. One can at the same time be an actor and an observer. Moreover, in paying no attention to the laws that govern reality dream allows temporal and physical expansions and condensations, and all this with an intrinsic naturalness that causes the dreamer to overlook the way dream defies the laws of nature and probability. Dream's power of condensation allows an object to be two things at once, such as when Gregor is both a man and a beast. Dream's capacity for expansion allows Bucephalus to be alive with Alexander and to cross over time and study our ancient tomes; expansion causes the emperor's messenger to traverse forever the distance that separates us from the emperor himself.

Condensation often works, as with Gregor, to suspend the laws of noncontradiction, often a semantic question, whereas expansion frequently correlates with Kafka's elaboration of the distance that separates the message from the receiver, or the searcher from the law. Dream provides, I stress, techniques for expression, and not in any special sense the content of Kafka's work, and this is true of Kafka's work from the beginning. The unmotivated embedding of different narratives in "Description of a Struggle" certainly has an irrational side to it that could be likened to the way dream can endlessly expand narration from within. In one of the best recent essays on this story Jost Schillemeid uses the terminology of dream analysis to describe the narrative progression as one that moves like an inner odyssey through an arbitrary dreamscape and pops out suddenly in the world of waking consciousness.[16]

The same temptation to use dream technique is evident in Kafka's second extant work, "Wedding Preparations in the Country." Its protagonist, Raban, plans to send his body out to the country while he remains in bed. Raban needs to find a way around the law of the excluded middle so that he can get out of the prototypical Kafkan dilemma—crossing the space that leads to the wedding altar. Dream technique may save him, but this is not certain. One recalls that, if the earlier "Description of a Struggle" narrates a dream odyssey, it also shows that the hero, like Ulysses, can nearly get lost in his dream travels and run the risk of never returning home again.

I stress this ambiguity, for, unlike the surrealists Kafka certainly never proposed that dream was a road to the absolute, to paraphrase one received view of surrealism's goal. Dream rhetoric provides a means for exploration, such as that which we see in several examples in *Meditation*, Kafka's first published book. The blurring of lines between objective and subjective worlds that Musil saw in this book represents Kafka's intuitive attempt to create a narrative space in which the laws of empirical reality do not limit his exploration. Dream techniques offer models of how the writer can place these laws in abeyance.

It is this dream quality of the verdict in "The Judgment" that makes the story so compelling. The story is at once a nightmare and, *as* a nightmare, a self-referential allegory about attempts to communicate across the space of trauma. Perhaps even more powerful in this respect is "The Metamorphosis." One must be attentive in using the concept of dream rhetoric here, for the inexperienced reader may be tempted to reduce the story dismissively to nothing but the tale of a bad dream. This interpretation is not entirely inadequate (though the plasticity of Kafka's open allegories is such that few interpretations can be entirely inadequate). But from the moment that Kafka sets Gregor's clock in accelerated motion it is clear that dream technique is being used here to put in question the very notion of identity. In waking reality we are supposedly what we are and not what we are not. But in dream we can be what we are and what we are not—A and not-A, as a logician might say. Dream technique thus allows Kafka to express what he takes to be a fundamental condition that the laws of empirical reality would exclude from narration, to wit, that by the law within us we are judged to be at once men and animals, mutually exclusive conditions. Accelerating clocks begin the process of condensation that leads to the final contradictory statement that Gregor is and is not Gregor. For condensation means the same object can have a multitude of meanings or identities, even contradictory ones.

These considerations of dream can be applied to a good many of the pieces of the *Nachlass*, and they would also apply to that extraordinary invention of "In the Penal Colony," the writing machine that is a literal condensation of several semantic notions and gives a good example of what Freud meant by condensation in his *Interpretation of Dreams*. Notions suggested by language become concrete objects in dream space. Kafka's exploration of dream comes to something of a culmination around 1917, during the time he wrote the stories for *A Country Doctor* (published in 1919). This is not to say that later works do not incorporate some aspects of dream rhetoric, but rather that the collection's title story, "A Country Doctor," is probably Kafka's richest exploration of dream techniques. As Hartmut Binder has observed about the story in his useful commentary on Kafka's short fiction, Kafka uses dream techniques in overcoming distances as if one were in a fairy tale; he uses them for the changing of perceptions in ways that would be impossible in the empirical world; and, finally, by suppressing paragraphs Kafka makes all events flow into each other, without any separation, as if in a dreamlike fusion of episodes.[17] Even at the most basic narrative level, then, Kafka uses dream rhetoric to meld together events so that the story's play of condensation and expansion acquires a dreamlike naturalization. For what is more "natural"—in Kafka at least—than to leave on a journey from which one will never return?

In this story the first-person narrator, a country doctor, explains that he must see an urgent case in a distant village. His horse is dead, however, and nobody will loan him one. When he kicks open the door of a long disused pigsty, he discovers a groom, ready with two powerful horses to hitch to his wagon. Virtually powerless to control the horses, the doctor flies into the night. As he leaves, he hears the animal-like groom breaking down the door of his house, where the groom sets about ravaging the doctor's serving girl. Ten miles are covered in a second. When he arrives, the doctor is carried from the gig into a house where he finds himself looking at a patient who wants to die. Lost in meditation the doctor cannot take his mind off the servant girl, while, as if to remind him of the presence of beasts in the world, the horses push their heads through the window. The doctor examines the sick boy and first believes that he is healthy. Then, as the horses whinny together, the doctor discovers a wound as big as the palm of his hand, with worms in it, a wound like a blossom that is destroying the boy.

The doctor laments about his impossible situation because the people expect him to replace the priest with his doctor's "omnipotence." Disappointed, however, the people strip the doctor of his clothes and lay him in bed with the boy. To make his escape the doctor finally gathers up his clothes, leaps on the gig, and commands the powerful beasts to flee—only to find that the space he must cross has expanded into infinite snowy wastes that he can never traverse:

> Never shall I reach home at this rate; my flourishing practice is done
> for; my successor is robbing me, but in vain, for he cannot take my
> place; in my house the disgusting groom is raging; Rose is his victim;
> I do not want to think about it anymore. Naked, exposed to the frost
> of this most unhappy of ages, with an earthly vehicle, unearthly

horses, old man that I am, I wander astray. My fur coat is hanging from the back of the gig, but I cannot reach it, and none of my limber pack of patients lifts a finger. Betrayed! Betrayed! A false alarm on the night bell once answered—it cannot be made good, not ever. (225)

And with these final lines the doctor is left adrift on Kafka's space of infinite expansion.

The very last lines ring out with the curious sound of a platitude; it is a noteworthy feature of this story that Kafka has embedded a series of clichés, proverbs, and even limericks into the fantastic narrative. When the doctor kicks open the pigsty and finds the groom on all fours there, his servant girl notes with classic understatement that "You never know what you're going to find in your own house" (220). Later, lamenting that the villagers would not loan him a horse, he philosophizes banally that "To write prescriptions is easy, but to come to an understanding with people is hard" (223). More expressionistically, in comforting the boy about the wound he received from an ax, the doctor seems to invent a proverb, "Many a one proffers his side and can hardly hear the ax in the forest, far less that it is coming nearer to him" (225). These bizarre platitudes, like bits of wisdom fixed by time immemorial, act like nodal points in the text around which the absurd events crystallize. In effect, these fixed units of sententious meaning resemble ironic condensations. They are condensations of woefully inadequate interpretations that Kafka contrasts with the absurd linking of events that leaves the doctor in the lurch. And though after reading this story nobody will ever wish to answer a false alarm again, it hardly seems that this final maxim can provide much of a guide for anyone wishing to return home across the snowy wastes of textual expansion.

Kafka uses this contrasting of ironic condensation and absurd linking of events to create another open allegory (by open allegory I mean a symbolic structure in which one term is fixed so as to allow, if not invite, the reader to apply multiple symbolic readings to that term). This allegory is evident in the extraordinary first paragraph in which the doctor finds that his horse is dead at the very moment he wishes to leave, that in the great drifts of snow it is pointless to seek to borrow one, and then that an animal-like groom is waiting for him in the pigsty, crouched on all fours. These events defying normal probability offer possibilities for semantic expansion in the sense that one can use several allegorical frameworks to explain them. One asks where, in symbolic terms, is the setting? in whose house? in a psychic space? in a metaphysical realm? are psychological projections occurring?

All of these questions can find plausible answers, especially if we respect Kafka's ironic reminder that "you never know what you have in your own house." The banality of the proverb also serves to point up a first level banality of the kind of interpretation that is "true" but inadequate. For the sudden presence of the lecherous groom and his horses truly demonstrates that one does not always know what one has in one's house, but truth is clearly not a sufficient condition for adequacy of interpretation. In this perspective it appears that it is not an accident that Kafka's hero is a doctor, for a doctor, as a clinician, is an interpreter of signs, quite literally a semiologist; in this story he must also interpret what is happening to him as he is pulled into the night by wild horses. His situation is, then, analogous to that of every dreamer or reader. In offering his banal interpretations he doubles for the reader who must interpret the good doctor's interpretations; hermeneutics is never far away in Kafka.

The doctor also lives in a social reality in which people are, as he puts it, always expecting the impossible from the doctor: "They have lost their ancient beliefs; the parson sits at home and unravels his vestments, one after another; but the doctor is supposed to be omnipotent with his merciful surgeon's hand" (224). The fall from religion to medicine is another expression of the fall into history and secular ways, that is, uncertain ways of dealing with experience. The ending could be read in this sense: having set out to bring comfort and certainty, the doctor finds himself lost in the infinite space that nothing in medicine (or semiology) has prepared him to cross.

The doctor is then another of Kafka's figures, who, like the arrow in the logical paradox of Zeno, flies but cannot move through space. Logical paradox and dream vision overlap in "A Country Doctor"—as they do in brief texts like "The Next Village" or "An Imperial Message"—to create a space that proliferates as quickly as one attempts to cross it. A more elaborate image of expansion is offered by the text "Up in the Gallery." In this parable a circus visitor watches the *Kunstreiterin*, the circus rider or "female artistic rider," who appears as if she might ride for months without stopping. And if this were to happen, the narrator says, then after months of this the gallery visitor, the dreamer, might run down and stop her—though to what end? But this is not the case, as the narrator then says. For the circus director enters the ring, accompanies her, and exults before her *Kunstfertigkeit*—her "unbelievable art-istry." The circus director, and not the visitor, lifts her in triumph, a triumph that has as a consequence that "the visitor to the gallery lays his face on the rail before him and, sinking into the closing march as into a heavy dream, weeps without knowing it" (402). Here the dreamer has dreamed first of an infinite expansion that might appear to be the dream of art without end, although the closure of the circus act brings about another dream, perhaps a dream within a dream. This dream might be a palliative for the pain we feel when art promises, but does not deliver, some fullness, even if only in the form of a circus show.

In other stories Kafka engages in comic play with dream rhetoric more explicitly than he does in "A Country Doctor." In "The Cares of a Family Man" Kafka gives us a father figure who is, quite properly it would seem, concerned about the existence of an "Odradek" that fre-quently comes to live in his house. The father must first explain to the reader the nature of this bizarre word he uses. It may be, according to some, of Slavonic origin, or, according to others, of Germanic prove-nance. With the father's explanation Kafka has anticipated what every reader will attempt to do when facing a term that vaguely suggests some anagram. In fact critics with a knowledge of Czech have not hes-itated to propose various readings (such as "fatherless," "miscreant," "a being outside of order," "poltergeist," or the imperative "stay away from me").[18] All of these seem equally plausible. But one must also take into account the comic play of dream rhetoric here, for it strikes me that Kafka has created a kind of censured term, playfully suggest-ing that the word has condensed into itself many possible meanings, much in the way Freud described the function of condensation in his work on the interpretation of dreams. Kafka's intent may well have been parodic; the effect certainly is.

The father must deal with a bizarre word, a dream condensation of many meanings that are censured and, if we were to follow Freud, are therefore accessible to the mind only in a scrambled form. But within the space of the story there is also a referent for the word. After all, as the narrator asks, who would undertake philology "if there were not a creature called Odradek"? (428). The living beast, condensing various meanings in his name, acts like a dysfunctional toy, an object without purpose, for it does not have "some kind of aim in life, some kind of activity" that could wear out. Hence the father speculates that it may be immortal, capable of surviving across the expanses of dream-time beyond the narrator's own life span. As such, the creature is an offense to the father, an insult to the role of the father and all that the father stands for—which is perhaps why the creature can only have a censured name. It can escape the father's law only as a ciphered form, since the law would refuse to recognize, indeed would condemn whatever an Odradek is (and I would suggest the obvious German *Dreck* is somewhere in there). The intolerable presence of an offensive Odradek shows that even the power of the superego has limits.

"The Cares of a Family Man" is a comedy directed at the father, which also seems to be the case of the story "Eleven Sons," a story that I find best read as a stand-up comedian's monologue. The father narrator's judgments of his sons turn back upon him as another comic demonstration of paternal limits. In both "Cares of a Family Man" and "Eleven Sons" Kafka uses comic techniques to circumvent the paternal power to which he paid homage in 1919 with "Letter to His Father."

Kafka borrowed from dream rhetoric in different ways in the two penultimate stories in *A Country Doctor*, "A Fratricide" and "A Dream." At first "A Fratricide" reads something like a police report: it is a brief description of a brutal murder, or perhaps a nightmare expressing some will to violence. One is certainly unsettled by the murderer's direct outpouring of joy, for Kafka allows his assassin, Schmar, to sing out his happiness upon stabbing to death his friend, Wese: "The bliss of murder! The relief, the soaring ecstasy from the shedding of another's blood! Wese, old nightbird, friend, alehouse crony, you are oozing away into the dark earth below the street. Why aren't you simply a bladder of blood so that I could stamp on you and make you vanish into nothingness. Not all we want comes true, not all the dreams that blossomed have borne fruit, your solid remains lie here. . ." (403–4). Kafka is, on the one hand, narrating an expressionist nightmare that draws upon dream's capacity to narrate the grotesque and the unacceptable as a natural occurrence. And, on the other hand, he has also created a rather elaborate literary conceit that is not immediately apparent, perhaps no more apparent than the symbolic underpinnings that are often attributed to dream.

The murderer who cries out these words is named Schmar, a name that appears to be a distorted version of *Smarh*, a work written by Flaubert during his youth (and Kafka's admiration of the French realist writer was virtually limitless). Flaubert's work is an immature imitation of Goethe's *Faust*, of which the young writer was well aware since he condemns himself at the end of *Smarh* for being a "little Goethe." The reference to Goethe sends the reader back to Kafka's tale in which Schmar's reference to blossoms that do not bloom is an indirect quotation from one of Goethe's most famous poems, "Prometheus." The line comes from the passage in which Prometheus, speaking with scorn to Zeus, asks ironically if he should hate life because not all dreams blossom to maturity. Kafka seems to be indulging in rather ferocious black humor here, narrating a dream-inversion of Prometheus as a murderer who has escaped from sensationalist fiction. The conceit involving two of Kafka's literary mentors takes away none of the violence of this expressionistic nightmare, though it does point up the kind of ironic control Kafka exerts over his work. Using Goethe to buttress the grotesque claims of a murderer is an extreme case of Kafka's intertextual play.

I am not certain as to why Kafka called this tale "A Fratricide," unless he wished to stress that all murders are repetitions of the original biblical fratricide that makes killing a brother the first and archetypical crime. By contrast, "A Dream" has exemplary clarity for a title: it narrates a dream. It is a dream of the hero of the posthumously published novel *The Trial*, Joseph K., the condemned man who, at the end of the novel, is taken away and murdered like a dog. "A Fratricide" is indirectly related to "A Dream," not only because it is Joseph K.'s fate in the novel to be murdered in a nightmarish way, but also because there is an image that is common to both stories, the image of a grass-covered grave. In "A Fratricide" when Madame Wese collapses on the body of her murdered husband, Kafka describes her fall by saying that "the nightgowned body belonged to Wese, the fur coat spreading over the couple like the smooth turf (*Rasen*) of a grave belonged to the crowd" (404). In Joseph K.'s dream he comes across a grave—his own—covered with grass; whereas in "A Fratricide" the fur coat is transformed, metaphorically, into the grass of the grave that has opened for Wese as he walks through the nightmarish streets of a murderer's dream. Joseph K. finds within his own dream a grass-covered hole into which he stumbles as if stumbling onto a promised revelation.

This common image of the grave points to Kafka's using the short story as a way of encountering, and perhaps countering the fascination worked by his dream of death. In "A Dream" Kafka clearly imitates dream by drawing upon the techniques of expansion and condensation to describe Joseph K.'s movement. He first sees a grave mound at a great distance, but then suddenly finds that with two steps he has nearly rushed beyond it. He comes, with an accelerating tempo, to a place of celebration where two men put up a gravestone, and when a third person appears, K. recognizes him as an artist.

The artist appears here with an ordinary pencil in order to write "golden letters." With these letters the artist has apparently come to engrave the final word about Joseph K.'s destiny. Perhaps his destiny is to know some form of salvation, for when the artist has, after some moments of difficulty, finally begun to engrave—and after a bell has rung—Joseph K. feels an *Erlösung*, a term for "relief" but also for "redemption" or "salvation." Joseph K. does not realize that the engraving is for his own tombstone until he sees the first line and then digs into the earth and discovers the great hole hiding beneath the grass and the earth's crust. As he sinks into the ground, he sees his name taking shape "across the stone above him in great flourishes" (401). Then he awakens. The dream has granted him one brief contact with the Word, engraved as a revelation, but this ephemeral contact is followed by the fall into darkness. Does the dream suggest that it is only here that contact with the Word, or at least the artist's revelation of it, can be had? But the dream also carries Joseph K.'s fall with it, and his awakening provides an escape from the fall. In the larger context provided by *The Trial*, however, awakening is no solution, since it is upon awakening one morning that Joseph K. finds himself arrested. Bad dreams can continue beyond sleep.

Falling and burrowing into the earth recur several times in Kafka's work, and the psychoanalytically inclined reader will see in this motif some reference to archetypal patterns. Burrowing does reproduce a frequent dream situation, and I think this notion applies to the last story I wish to consider here, "A Visit to a Mine." At first this piece seems to be based on a realistic description of working conditions in a mine (and Kafka's work did make him familiar with such scenes). But, as in dream, the real is incorporated in a framework that imposes on it a fantasy distortion. The narrator, a worker down in the bowels of a deep mine, reports on the visit of the "highest engineers" when they visit new tunnels under construction. Kafka presents a fantastic parade of engineers—ten to be exact—followed by one "servant" or office porter. (One wonders if there is some affinity between this group of eleven and the eleven sons of the father's monologue.) In his description of the engineers the narrator lists their capacities, the knowledge they possess, the techniques that make them superior beings who inhabit some realm that "we," the workers in the mine, can never know: "We fancy that we know our mine and its rock formations, but what this engineer can be sounding all the time in such a manner lies beyond our comprehension" (406). Seen from the narrator's perspective of blind admiration, the engineers appear a comically fantastic group of men possessing a problematic knowledge.

In this respect they are not unlike the keepers of the law and can be likened to a dream displacement of Kafka's judges. "A Visit to a Mine" also expresses the dreams of knowledge we frequently have, as when, we know in dreams that total knowledge is present, knowledge that might explain all, but which we cannot bring back to our waking consciousness. Wandering in the tunnels, Kafka's recurrent image of the labyrinthine expansion of space, the engineers must hold some knowledge or vision that is beyond our daily competence, otherwise, we reason, why would they exist (much like Kafka's characters who reason that the law must exist if they are condemned)? And so we think that we know that they know, even if they are followed by a porter pulling a perambulator with its enigmatic instrument, supposedly for garnering even more unknown knowledge. We laugh at him even as we find he is "an unsolved riddle for us to respect" (407). Perhaps from Kafka's exploration of what lies on the other side of what we think we know this unsolved riddle is the final message that dreams bring us.

A *Hunger Artist*

In 1924, as he was dying, Kafka corrected the proofs for *A Hunger Artist*, a collection of four stories. Three of these clearly deal with the image of the artist, and the fourth, "A Little Woman," has been interpreted as an allegory about Kafka's writing.[19] In this chapter I focus on the three stories, "First Sorrow," "A Hunger Artist," and "Josephine the Singer, or the Mouse Folk," in order to discuss the ways in which they deal with Kafka's views of the artist and art. The question of the artist and the function of art underlies nearly all of Kafka's work insofar as his work interrogates itself about its own meaning and the possibility of communication. In these later stories, however, Kafka displaces this interrogation in that he writes explicitly about several types of artists— trapeze artist, master faster, or mouse cantatrice—and these stories reflect not only upon his work, but upon the artist in a more general sense. The characters complete a gallery of types of artists that Kafka began creating earlier, especially in the circus rider of *A Country Doctor* and, most notably, the talking ape of "A Report to an Academy," about which I shall say something presently.

The notion of the "artist" in postromantic Germany could still conjure up the image of a creative demiurge, though Kafka's artists hardly fit this description. They are more likely to call forth a snicker. Kafka is hardly the first writer to present the artist as a laughter-provoking beast hardly worthy of serious consideration; I ask the reader to consider the following lamentation about the poet's plight by a romantic writer whom Kafka read with the greatest interest, E.T.A. Hoffmann: "Once glowed in the breast of the chosen ones the inner, holy striving to express in glorious words that which they had most deeply felt; and even those who had not been chosen had belief and devotion; they honored poets as prophets who could prophesy of a glorious unknown world full of shining riches; and they did not suppose that those who weren't elected might be able to enter that holy realm about which poetry gave them a distant annunciation. Now everything has changed."[20] The romantic Hoffmann thus offers at once a description of both the artist's task and the remote period when the artist could accomplish that task, all of which is couched in a complaint about the present day's fall from that glorious past. This is a familiar historical configuration. Once things were different; the poet-prophet could enter the superior realm of the sacred and the ideal. But that moment has been lost. It might appear that, as modern philosophers such as Heidegger or Derrida would have it, poets *always* find themselves as those who *once* had access to a sacred sphere, that once there was no fallenness. But in the present moment artists have "always already" undergone a fall from some moment of privileged annunciation. Or as Kafka put it in his views on our fall into history, poets are always repeating the past's decline. They live it as an eternal repetition in the present.

Hoffmann goes one step further in dramatizing this lamentation, and this is the step that interested Kafka. Hoffmann's speaker, complaining about the difference between then and now, is a dog. He is, to be sure, a rather famous dog, the Berganza that Cervantes first described in a story about his conversations with Scipion (in his *Novelas ejemplares* or *Exemplary Tales*) and whose adventures Hoffmann continued in his tale called "Nachricht von den neuesten Schicksalen des Hundes Berganza" ("Report on the latest Fate of the Dog Berganza"). The dog Berganza, like Kafka's horse Bucephalus, is well placed to report on the fall, for this canine has lived several centuries, and in his latest avatar, I think, he has become Kafka's beast artist and thinker of the twentieth century.

Reports on the fall—the fall from true humanity—are appropriately made by dogs and apes and other utterly fallen artists. We have already seen some of these fallen or degraded artists in Kafka's earlier work in which beasts are looking for knowledge and redemption, such as "Investigations of a Dog" (written in 1922, at the same time as the tales in *A Hunger Artist*), or, even more obliquely, in "The Metamorphosis." One of Kafka's most remarkable portrayals of the artist as beast is found in a piece he published in *A Country Doctor,* "A Report to the Academy." On reading this tale narrated by an ape, one immediately wants to draw analogies with James Joyce's portrait of the artist as a young man and the later portrait of the artist as a young monkey by Michel Butor, for Kafka's portrait is situated clearly in a development that leads from a view of the artist as a heroic forger of myth to one of the artist as a dealer in aping junk. But the best starting point for looking at intertextual affinities is again a romantic text, again by Hoffmann, namely his fantasy piece called "Nachricht von einem gebildeten jungen Mann" ("Report from a Cultured Young Man") which contains a letter from Milos, a well-educated ape, to his friend Pipi in North America. Hoffmann's primate has learned to ape all the mannerisms of Europeans of good education and has become a consummate artistic charlatan merely by using the instinct for imitation that causes us to laugh at apes—and which we say is the basis of our art. From the time of Aristotle to the present day Western art has constantly returned to mimesis—imitation and representation—as the basis for its existence; therefore, if the artist is an imitator, he is, as Hoffmann and, even more pointedly, Kafka show, quite literally an ape.

Kafka's ape narrator in "A Report to the Academy" is also a product of a long history, to wit, the history of the ascent of man that Darwin told in his version of the origin of the species. Kafka's ironies about art and science leave one uncertain as to whether he is presenting man as an elevated ape, or his ape as a fallen man. In any case, in Kafka's tale the well-educated ape finds that his instinct for imitation is a part of a historical process for which he must give an account; Kafka's ape is in fact reporting on his origins—the origins of a, if not the, species of ape artists—and in this respect Kafka offers the artist as a strange culmination of one of nature's more bizarre evolutionary branchings.

Beyond Darwin, Kafka's parody aims at the myth of origins itself, at that myth that would assign some end to the retrospective expansion we can create as the tale of our history. Origins are always already given by the desire to construct a limit for the distances we see behind us; or, as Kafka's ape narrator says, in pointing out the arbitrary nature of these creations: "It is now nearly five years since I was an ape, a short space of time, perhaps, according to the calendar, but an infinitely long time to gallop through at full speed, as I have done. . . ." (250). Yet we all believe that in some sense we are still tied as apes to that long trip that took us from our origins, over evolutionary distances, to the present moment: "To put it plainly . . . your life as apes, gentlemen, insofar as something of that kind lies behind you, cannot be farther removed from you than mine is from me. Yet everyone on earth feels a tickling at the heels; the small chimpanzee and the great Achilles alike" (250). Our animal origins remain with us, and perhaps man—or the Kafkan artist—can only exist as a beast. Kafka's ape, like all of us apparently, has become or tried to become a man by imitating what a man is. He has aped man, has followed his animal instinct for imitation, so that paradoxically he becomes a man by using his skills as an ape.

There is one noteworthy if subtle difference between Kafka the artist and his aping creation, for Kafka's correspondence and diaries reveal
that his greatest agony was that he could not find the freedom to be,
in the simplest terms, himself, that is, the artist he longed to be. The
ape who imitates man, on the other hand, claims that he did not begin
imitating in order to gain his freedom once he was captured; rather, he
merely wanted an *Ausweg*, a way out: "I deliberately do not use the
word 'freedom' . . . may I say that all too often men are betrayed by
the word freedom. And as freedom is counted among the most sublime
feelings, so the corresponding disillusionment can be also sublime"
(253). For the ape has observed freedom in art and has become
disillusioned:

> In variety theaters I have often watched, before my turn came on, a
> couple of acrobats performing on trapezes high in the roof. They
> swung themselves, they rocked to and fro, they sprang into the air,
> they floated into each other's arms, one hung by the hair from the
> teeth of the other. "And that too is human freedom," I thought,
> "self-controlled movement." What a mockery of holy Mother Na-
> ture! Were the apes to see such a spectacle, no theater walls could
> stand the shock of their laughter. (253)

The ape sees our artists as practitioners in freedom, but in their human
freedom they are a distortion of nature, a comic deviation that, in some
sense, marks art for Kafka as a kind of derisive activity, sacred and
risible at the same time.

The trapeze artist, the circus equestrienne, and the writer all use or
practice freedom, but they are all deviants with regard to pure nature:
freedom is a superfluous notion for a natural being. Our ape narrator,
half human artist, half mimicking animal, retains a memory of a nature
that asks for none of the redundant gestures of freedom, or the dubious
doublings of mimesis. The natural being, like the sister at the end of
"The Metamorphosis" or the panther that replaces the artist in star-
vation at the end of "A Hunger Artist," has a body that bursts with
sufficiency, that has no need of the freedom that the artists need. The
caged panther, for instance, "seemed not even to miss his freedom;
his noble body, furnished almost to the bursting point with all that it
needed, seemed to carry freedom around with it too; somewhere in his
jaws it seemed to lurk" (277). The self-sufficiency of the natural world,
like a paradise from which we are forever driven, remains in the back

of our ape's mind; and once this ape has been put in his cage in Africa, the most he can desire is a way out: he decides to become an artist.

As Kafka portrays the ape in "A Report to the Academy," he becomes an artist who practices Aristotle's *Poetics* by imitating what he sees about him:

> What a triumph it was . . . when one evening before a large circle of spectators—perhaps there was a celebration of some kind, a gramophone was playing, an officer was circulating among the crew—when on this evening, just as no one was looking, I took hold of a schnapps bottle that had been carelessly left standing before my cage, uncorked it in the best style, while the company began to watch me with mounting attention, set it to my lips without hesitation, with no grimace, like a professional drinker, with rolling eyes and full throat, actually and truly drank it empty; then threw the bottle away, not this time in despair but as an artistic performer. (257)

With this acting performance he breaks into speech and into the human community. The way out leads then from Zoological Garden to the variety stage and, on the way, leaving his apedom behind, he can reach the cultural level of the average European. Having attained this level, the ape-artist, now a comically redundant expression, can take up a proto-Kafkan position and sit by the window in his rocking chair and gaze out on that exterior world to which he is a stranger.[21]

Kafka's ape is metamorphosed into an ironic representative of a poetic tradition that once vouchsafed the greatest philosophical seriousness to aping, and his sitting by the window figures the kind of alienation the modern artist feels in looking back on that tradition that believed imitation brought one into the realm of nature. Moreover, the tale is one of several in which Kafka seems to take pleasure in revealing that the artist is, if not a deviant, then a superfluous being whose work can just as well be done by mere imaginings, with no need for concrete realization. This minimalist strategy underlies, for example, the anticipation of conceptual art that Kafka offers in "The City Coat of Arms," a later parable written two years before "Investigations of a Dog." This exemplary text begins by saying that all was going well in the construction of the Tower of Babel, perhaps too well, since people thought more about "guides, interpreters, accommodations for the workmen, and roads of communication" (433) than about actually building the tower up to the heavens: "People argued in this way: The essential thing in the whole business is the idea of building a tower that will reach to heaven. In comparison with that idea everything else is secondary. The idea, once seized in its magnitude, can never vanish again. . ." (433).

Baukunst—or architecture, as the emblem of all arts—is reduced to a mere conceptual matter. It matters little if the edifice is ever built, since that would entail the haphazard material manifestation of the idea (every century will have its own building techniques, and usually better ones as time goes by, so why be in a hurry?). Kafka pushes the idea of mimesis to a kind of absurdly logical conclusion: if art imitates the idea or ideal, the artist need not bother with the derivative act of imitation, since the idea continues to exist independently. The idea needs no material embodiment, since, as with the concept of the Tower of Babel, it can circulate freely and traverse great historical expanses of time that, in fact, the realized work could never cross. The idea of the Tower of Babel can, for example, pop up in a parable by a German language writer living in Prague at the beginning of the twentieth century. The concept of the tower is clearly contained therein, even if the parable exists to explain the nonexistence of the material realization of the concept, which can then take on other, variant forms of nonexistence, such as the pit of Babylon that Kafka saw as a project that one might have burrowed into existence (*PP*, 37).

If the artist's creation is at best apery, and in any case a derivative act better left undone, then the artist is thrown back upon himself to find some reason for his existence. Denied recourse to some problematic exterior realm of the ideal, he is obliged to look within himself and find the sources of art in his innards. In a sense all that is left to him is to discourse on his own condition and literally to turn himself into art—as Kafka shows in "First Sorrow," and especially in his initiation into body art, "A Hunger Artist." Art here is the process of art, which is to say, art feeds on the mere process of the artist being an artist. Or one might say that Kafka's idea of art is minimalism with a vengeance: the artistic process is the act that can lead to the disappearance of the artist.

The first story in *A Hunger Artist* is "First Sorrow," the tale of the initiation into suffering of the fanatical trapeze artist who is the story's protagonist. Swinging on a trapeze is of course a nonmimetic art and offers an ambivalent image of art as a trivial if intense process. Kafka's choice of circus artist is ambivalent in that it seems to stand for the kind of fallen status of the artist at the same time that it suggests that the artist can be found anywhere, perhaps everywhere—always already about to fall into our midsts. Living on the margins of culture, his trapeze artist is not just an acrobat who turns his body into art: he is an artist who does nothing else. Kafka is again pursuing his absurd logic to a reasonable conclusion. For if the artist is an artist only insofar as he practices his art—a proposition that Kafka entertained in several contexts—then the only way to exist as an artist is always to be an artist, that is, never to stop. So the trapeze artist never comes down from his exalted position "high in the vaulted domes of the great variety theaters" (446). Day and night he stays on his trapeze. Given this rather extraordinary opening premise for the story, the story then unfolds "realistically" by telling what must be done for the artist to exist. He must eat, he sees people now and then, and he constantly performs. Only unavoidable travel occasionally interrupts this routine.

Travel is the distraction from art—and what could one expect from the writer who lives Zeno's paradox? It marks a moment when the artist is not keeping "his art at the pitch of perfection," (446) at its *Vollkommenheit*. Not surprisingly, then, it is during a voyage that the trapeze artist comes up with a new idea. While dreaming he decides he must henceforth have two trapezes for his performances, one next to the other. And with this demand the rather petulant artist begins to cry, even though his impresario readily agrees with him.

In a dream the trapeze artist finds the desire to double his art and, with this desire for doubling he knows his first *Leid*, sorrow and suffering. I wonder if this image of one trapeze next to the other does not convey a sense of art that, like Kafka's, feeds on itself by representing itself. The artist wants to double his performance, and self-doubling is the essence of self-representation, which is to say that the artist knows his first sorrow in this moment when he is tempted by imitation, mimesis, and doubling. And I suppose one could plausibly argue that if the goal of art is imitation, what could a trapeze artist imitate except himself? Art, then, in its fullness as mimesis leads to sorrow and suffering, an idea Kafka himself expressed when he told Gustav Janouch that for the artist art is a suffering (*Leid*) through which he frees himself for a new suffering; and, I would add, not the least of which is the suffering he feels about his incapacity to represent anything except his suffering.[22]

The tale's final lines suggest that, with the complication of his art the trapeze artist has lost that childlike state of naive grace that has been a German way of describing the artist since at least the time

Schiller described Goethe as a product of nature: "Once such ideas began to torment him, would they ever quite leave him alone? Would they not rather increase in urgency? Would they not threaten his very existence? And indeed the manager believed he could see, during the apparently peaceful sleep which had succeeded the fit of tears, the first furrows of care engraving themselves upon the trapeze artist's smooth, childlike forehead" (448). Art as suffering is written on the artist's forehead, as it might be engraved on a stone. Does Kafka suggest the futility of doubling the artist's performance, since, in any case, art and its attendant suffering are only manifest in the body? The trapeze artist would then be a first cousin of Kafka's best known body artist, the fasting champion who gives this final collection its title.

The hunger artist, like the trapeze artist, never stops practicing his art. He would fast for days on end, even forever, if he could. He literally uses his body for his art. And in this process of ascesis he has the capacity to symbolize every artist hero from the Christian Creator, who allowed his body to be hung up on public display, to the body artists of the sixties and seventies who, subjecting their flesh to public demonstrations of sado-masochism, proclaimed they were the art of the immediate moment. Or, from another perspective, the hunger artist looks back to these performers of degraded spectacle that were once found in the circus and the music hall, the freaks and the misfits (and historically real hunger artists) who are another double of the fallen artist who can only use his own body for his art. Kafka probably never created a character capable of generating a richer allegory, at once both specific in its description of the artist, and capable of derisively portraying the structure of most of our beliefs in artistic revelation.

Fasting, like all art, has had a historical development—and that development can only take the form of a fall. Once popular, fasting has known the fate of all art forms or movements; it has lost audience favor, and as the story progresses, the reader sees the hunger artist relegated to the periphery of our culture, finally disappearing as his art form becomes incomprehensible. Of course, the reader never *sees* that moment of great popularity that fasting once knew. This moment can only be remembered, recalled by a narrator who begins the story by saying that "During these last decades the interest in professional fasting has markedly diminished"; and then goes on to say that the art pays little today in this world that is so different from the one in which people flocked to see hunger artists (268). Like Hoffmann's dog recalling those days when poet prophets were honored, the narrator of "A Hunger Artist" remembers a time when people were not revulsed by the hunger artist, when they "understood" him and his achievement. But, the reader will ask, was there a time when art was not already a victim of misunderstanding? For this is always (and already) the meaning of the present in Kafka's work.

The narrator, like the guardian of the machine of "In the Penal Colony," can claim to remember when the hunger artist would spend his forty days before appreciative crowds during the day, and then would be watched at night. At night, to allay suspicion that he might be eating, he would push his art even further, for "sometimes he mastered his feebleness sufficiently to sing during their watch for as long as he could keep going, to show them how unjust their suspicions were" (269). It would seem that the hunger artist was not entirely appreciated in those past days either, for the guards would react to his song by wondering how he could sing while putting food in his mouth. In one sense Kafka is giving a literal representation of the cliché about the "misunderstood artist," but with an ironic twist: this artist is truly misunderstood in that no one realizes that he cannot find the sustenance he needs, the sustenance that would free him from his miserable art. The hunger artist would, he says later, cease fasting if he were able to find a food he liked; so he must bear the watch of those who can, like healthy animals, fling themselves in the morning with keen appetite on the breakfast that the hunger artist buys for them.

Kafka is dramatizing the most minimal art here, the art of turning a lack of substance (or sustenance) into an art form. But for the artist who cannot find the sustenance he wants this is not a difficult task, though his audience may not wish to believe it: "For he alone knew, what no other initiate knew, how easy it was to fast. It was the easiest thing in the world. He made no secret of this, yet people did not believe him, at the best they set him down as modest, most of them, however, thought he was out for publicity or else was some kind of cheat who found it easy to fast because he had discovered a way of making it easy, and then had the impudence to admit the fact, more or less" (270). I quote the above lines because it seems to me there is something devastating about the way Kafka, with an ironic smile, admits that starving is the easiest thing in the world. Starving is easy, and within the right framework—in a cage or a book—we can then look upon it as art. And while I do not wish to run the risk of inflating the importance of my subject—though this hardly seems possible when dealing with Kafka—Kafka appears here to be anticipating the total disarray of our current literary and artistic scene; with incomparably more irony and self-awareness than most of today's artists, he outlines the position of the artist as the fraudulent, the necessarily if haplessly fraudulent minimalist.

The changing historical understanding of art, the changing artistic fashions as it were, gives the hunger artist the opportunity to show the ease with which he fasts, though nobody is likely to be concerned with his record-setting performance. Since the hunger artist can no longer attract "today" the crowds he once did, he can no longer work alone. But a large circus agrees to take him on and places his cage near the animal cages, on a concourse that the public uses in going to and from the main attraction. He thus finds himself unwittingly in competition with the animals as a spectacle. When the way is blocked in front of his cage, people stop; fathers even remember for their children the great feats of hunger artists, but this is of little interest to the children. To increase his alienation, the hunger artist must suffer the nauseating stench of the raw meat that the keepers bring to feed the beasts of prey.

Ignored by the public, finally forgotten by the circus management, the artist fasts on and on until one day an overseer wonders why there is an empty cage standing about unused. The hunger artist has fasted himself into near invisibility. And it is at that moment that we learn that he is another of Kafka's protagonists who, for lack of sustenance, is withering away in spite of himself. As he dies he tells the overseer that he should not be admired:

> "Because I have to fast, I can't help it," said the hunger artist. "What a fellow you are," said the overseer, "and why can't you help it?" "Because," said the hunger artist, lifting his head a little and speaking, with his lips pursed, as if for a kiss, right into the overseer's ear, so that no syllable might be lost, "because I couldn't find the food I liked. If I had found it, believe me, I should have made no fuss and stuffed myself like you or anyone else." These were his last words, but in his dimming eyes remained the firm though no longer proud persuasion that he was still continuing to fast. (277)

Like Gregor, the vermin of "The Metamorphosis," the hunger artist falls from language into silence and then death because he cannot find the sustenance he needs. The difference between vermin and artist may appear minimal in this awful perspective, but an even more extraordinary parallel is found in their last erotic gestures—Gregor reaches up to his sister with vermin tenderness, the hunger artist purses his emaciated lips "as if for a kiss." Moreover, Kafka ends each story with an image that presents the antithesis of a withered speechless beetle or an emaciated hunger artist; he presents the image of animal self-sufficiency that the sensual sister or the sleek panther proposes. I stress this parallel because it seems to me that these two stories complement each other not only in the way they show that hunger, speechlessness, and art are parts of the same configuration, but also in the way that their final image shows that the contrary of spiritual fulfillment in Kafka is mere animal plenitude. And this is another speechless state, a natural state devoid of the sin of self-consciousness. And, finally, art stands out clearly as belonging to those who practice it as a surrogate for something they cannot name, except perhaps negatively through art.

If one wished to argue that Kafka's stories anticipate virtually all the important literary and artistic currents that have emerged since World War II, then one could claim that his "Josephine the Singer, or the Mouse Folk," with all of Kafka's wry humor, sets out the premises of pop art. Pop art, I would say, proposes the ambivalent view that our modern culture has no art, and if this is the case, then everything is art, including Campbell Soup cans, neon signs, and advertising posters, and representations thereof. In Kafka's story his mouse folk seem to have little in the way of art, but their Josephine claims to be a singer. Yet the hostile narrator asks, what is it that makes her singing a song? All she appears to be doing is ordinary *pfeifen*, a verb the English translation makes into "piping," but it also means "whistling." Josephine whistles, and all mice do that. What justifies calling her piping "art"?

"Josephine" brings up the epistemological dilemma of art that has become the subject matter of much contemporary art: how do we know what art is? The story's narrator, another historian of the fall of art, says the mouse folk once did have art, but how, he asks, can one know what is art today? What can one say about Josephine's claim to sing?

> Is it in fact singing at all? Although we are unmusical we have a tradition of singing; in the old days our people did sing; this is mentioned in legends and some songs have actually survived, which, it is true, no one can now sing. Thus we have an inkling of what singing is, and Josephine's art does not really correspond to it. So is it singing at all? Is it not perhaps just a piping? And piping is some-

thing we all know about, it is the real artistic accomplishment of our people, or rather no mere accomplishment, but a characteristic expression of our life. We all pipe, but of course no one dreams of making out that our piping is an art. (361)

This deceptively dense passage brings up a number of questions about the nature of art. On the one hand, it obliges us to ask at what point we separate art from the everyday activities of normal life. This is an anthropological question that suggests that the separation of art and daily life already entails the loss of a meaningful function for art. And, on the other hand, the passage asks what allows us to designate some aspects of culture as art, and not others? This was the question that Marcel Duchamp asked at approximately the same time when he entered a well-formed urinal in an art show, though, with a sense of romantic individualness he differentiated it from all others by signing it "R. Mutt." Josephine's piping may well have the same kind of individuation; it is signed "Josephine." In and of itself, however, what can decide which whistling is art and which is not? Can a mere declaration of intent suffice to make something into a work of art? In the fifties and sixties some artists claimed that this was the case. Rauschenberg said that if he said so, a telegram could be a portrait. More pointedly, the Dutch artist Stanley Brouwn announced in 1960 that all the shoe shops in Amsterdam constituted an exhibition of his work.[23] Like Warhol's putting a soup can in a frame, does Josephine's appearance on a stage suffice to realize her intention: to transform everyday activity into whatever it is we mean by art?

For her part Josephine is convinced that more than her mere intent differentiates her piping from the ordinary squeaks of mousedom. But she also knows that art requires a framework that gives it a space that separates it from ordinary activities. The trapeze artist is an artist only when he is surrounded by space on his bar, the hunger artist is different from a run-of-the-mill starving person only when he is set off by the bars of his cage, and Josephine is a singer only when she is standing before a crowd whose silence is a necessary condition if her sounds are to be framed as art: "Since piping is one of our thoughtless habits, one might think that people would pipe up in Josephine's audience, too; her art makes us feel happy, and when we are happy we pipe; but her audience never pipes, it sits in mouselike stillness; as if we had become partakers in the peace we long for, from which our own piping at the very least holds us back, we make no sound" (362). Silence creates the paradoxical condition in which the mice entertain that their own whistling is something other than their whistling, and so they allow no one to pipe up: "Once it happened while Josephine was singing that some silly little thing in all innocence began to pipe up too. Now it was just the same as what we were hearing from Josephine; in front of us the piping sound that despite all rehearsal was still tentative and here in the audience the unself-conscious piping of a child; it would have been impossible to define the difference; but yet at once we hissed and whistled the interrupter down" (362–63).

Kafka's description of Josephine's performance presents us with a dazzling exercise in perspective viewing, much as if we were viewing one of those ambivalent designs that can alternately be a duck or a rabbit according to what one views as foreground or background in one's vision. Is Josephine doing exactly what all mice do in their normal whistling? Or is she giving a performance that *represents* exactly what they do all the time? I cannot avoid the feeling that this might be perfect mimesis—the imitation that is so exact that one cannot distinguish it from what is imitated. With more humor and less sense of scandal, Kafka obviously shares the astonishment that Pascal, that puritanical Jansenist, felt about the arts of imitation. Why, asked Pascal, would one admire in a representation what one would find a matter of indifference in reality?

Whatever the intrinsic nature of Josephine's art, it has an extrinsic appeal. She can command an audience to appear simply by letting the word circulate that she is going to sing. Processions then form, and, if necessary, messengers go out to guarantee a large audience. Hence, Josephine has a very high opinion of herself and her art, an opinion that is quite different from that of the narrator. Because she claims to have a social function, several critics have said that Josephine is a reflection of the young Zionists in Prague who saw themselves as capable of uniting the Jewish people. The flexible nature of Kafka's open allegory can certainly apply to any kind of situation in which the artist claims to serve the people, and this claim only makes more pointed the questions posed as to what art is in the first place. With regard to the social function of the artist, the story's narrator has a rather critical view, for he contends that it is the people who nurture the artist, and that "no single individual could do what in this respect the people as a whole are capable of doing" (365). It is the people who draw the individual in like a nurseling to protect her or him, even if Josephine believes on the contrary that "it is she who protects the people" (366).

The narrator flatly rejects, moreover, any prophetic or Messianic claims the artist may have: "she does not save us and she gives us no strength" (366). Yet almost contradictorily the narrator is willing to grant her art a minimal function, especially in times of crisis, although her social role proves, he claims, that she is no singer:

> This piping, which rises up where everyone else is pledged to silence, comes almost like a message from the whole people to each individual; Josephine's thin piping amidst grave decisions is almost like our people's precarious existence amidst the tumult of a hostile world. . . . A really trained singer, if ever such a one should be found among us, we could certainly not endure at such a time and we should unanimously turn away from the senselessness of any such performance. May Josephine be spared from perceiving that the mere fact of our listening to her is proof that she is no singer. (367–68)

Apparently art could lead the people only by not being art, which is to say something separate from their daily crises like the singing of a trained singer. The narrator is hardly more consistent than Josephine, however, in alternately granting her and refusing her some justification for her high opinion of her art. Perhaps in the end we can no more discern whether her art has a social function than we can know if it is art at all.

The narrator acts as a kind of dialectical foil to Josephine's defense and illustration of her art. And after discussing whether her art leads the people or vice versa, he describes again the nature of her art, this time in a way that sounds like a parodistic exposition of modernist aesthetics. For he finds that Josephine's appeal consists, in part, in the way that her piping restores, in the language of the people, something of the essence of time lost, of their "poor brief childhood," and of a "lost happiness that can never be found again" (370). If this sounds like a description of the function of art that Marcel Proust attributed to literature in his novel about seeking time past, the following lines about Josephine's singing sound like a rewriting of the symbolist poet Mallarmé's modernist views of poetic language: "Of course it is a kind of piping. Why not? Piping is our people's daily speech, only many a one pipes his whole life long and does not know it, where here piping is set free from the fetters of daily life and it sets us free too for a little while. We certainly should not want to do without these performances"

(370). Josephine's art, like Mallarmé's, sets piping free from the fetters of utilitarian usage, it takes the *parole brute*, or ordinary language, and frees it to be the *parole essentielle*, or essential language, of poetry. The analogy works in both directions, since Mallarmé, the high priest of poetic celebration, would have readily agreed that ordinary language is much like mouse squeaking.

In this waggish perspective the miracle of art is that such meaningless chirping could ever be converted into poetry—while remaining language. And this understanding of art demands one additional ironic appreciation, for "Josephine" is initially a product of poetry; specifically, she is first found in a rather sentimental poem by the nineteenth-century German poet Mörike. In Mörike's poem the poet hears the "heavenly harmony" of a Josephine singing at mass. Divinity, Mörike tells us, is found in Josephine's song; and perhaps it is so, for what or who can differentiate our ordinary chirping from essential revelation?

When refused special dispensation from work—and what artist does not need free time to perfect his or her art?—the mouse Josephine is reported to disappear at the story's end. Her abandoning the people receives typically ambivalent commentary from the narrator; he declares at once that she is a small episode in the history of his people and that it will not be easy for them to get over losing her. She will at once live on in their memory and be forgotten in the numberless throng of the heroes of the people. This is Kafka's final dialectic, a play of thesis and antithesis, worked out while he was dying, that constitutes the only approach to those truths that flee nonparadoxical affirmation. For Kafka's work itself is the kind of art that we feel at once we cannot live without, although his art demonstrates that we are not one step closer to any truth for having, like Josephine's people, let this piping resound in our silence. Yet, this is a truth, too, and it is the truth of a paradoxical wisdom that makes of Kafka, if not of Josephine, one of the few truly great artists of the twentieth century.

Notes

1. Marthe Robert would go so far as to maintain that Kafka never wrote about anything except the "tragic and derisive struggle that, without hope, the ancient and the new made within him" (*Livres des Lectures* [Paris: Grasset, 1977], 155).

2. *Sämtliche Erzählungen*, ed. Paul Raabe (Frankfurt: Fischer Taschenbuch, 1975), 209; hereafter cited in the text as R.

3. I note that a *Mowe*, or gull, flies through him in Version A; whereas *The Complete Stories* has little mosquitoes going through the poor fat man (29).

4. *The Complete Stories*, ed. N. N. Glatzer (New York: Schocken Books, 1971), 451; hereafter cited by page number in the text.

5. Jacques Derrida, "Before the Law," in *Kafka and the Contemporary Critical Performance*, ed. Alan Udoff (Bloomington: Indiana University Press, 1987), 140.

6. *Dearest Father: Stories and Other Writings*, trans. Ernst Kaiser and Eithne Wilkins (New York: Schocken Books, 1954), 320; also Gustav Janouch, *Gespräche mit Kafka*, expanded edition (Frankfurt: Fischer, 1968), 75.

7. There are in fact some changes in the version that Kafka actually published. This version is translated in *The Penal Colony* (New York: Schocken Books, 1948) but not in *The Complete Stories*. The quotation is from page 12; hereafter cited in the text as *PC*.

8. *Briefe, 1902–1924*, ed. Max Brod (Frankfurt: Fischer, 1975), 29.

9. Quoted in Richard Hayman, *Kafka: A Biography* (New York: Oxford University Press, 1982), 66.

10. Wilhelm Emrich, *Franz Kafka* (Frankfurt: Athenaeum, 1960), 127.

11. Stanley Corngold, *The Commentator's Despair* (Port Washington, N.Y.: Kennikat Press, 1973), 12.

12. There are several references to Freud in Kafka's letters and diaries. Perhaps the most revealing is to be found in *Briefe an Milena*, Expanded Edition, ed. Jürgen Born and Michael Muller (Frankfurt: Fischer, 1986), 292. Here Kafka explains what he sees as the theoretical error underlying psychoanalysis.

13. *Parables and Paradoxes* (New York: Schocken Books, 1946), 29; hereafter cited in the text as *PP*. See also *Dearest Father*, 41.

14. Letter quoted by Max Brod, *Der Prozess* (Frankfurt: Fischer, 1979), 194.

15. Gustav Janouch, *Gespräche mit Kafka*, 55–56.

16. Jost Schillemeid, "Kafkas *Beschreibung eines Kampes*. Ein Beitrag zum Textverstandnis und zur Geschichte von Kafkas," in *Der junge Kafka*, ed. Gerhard Kurz (Frankfurt: Suhrkamp, 1984), 111.

17. Hartmut Binder, *Kafka-Kommentar zu Sämtlichen Erzählungen* (Munich: Winkler Verlag, 1975), 210.

18. Hartmut Binder, *Kafka-Kommentar*, 232.

19. This interpretation of "A Little Woman" is to be found in Malcolm Pasley, "Kafka's Semi-private Games," *Oxford German Studies* 6 (1971–72):112–31. It is ingenuous, but not altogether convincing.

20. E. T. A. Hoffmann, "Nachricht von den neuesten Schicksalen des Hundes Berganza," in *E. T. A. Hoffmann's gesammelte Schriften.* ed. Theodor Hosemann, vol. 7 (Berlin: G. Reimer, 1871), 100–101. My translation.

21. Many critics see Kafka's ape as portraying the plight of the assimilated Jew in Europe. This is an interesting thesis, and perhaps complementary to my own interpretation.

22. Gustav Janouch, *Gespräche mit Kafka*, 34.

23. Robert Smith, "Conceptual Art," in *Concepts of Modern Art*, 2nd Edition, ed. Nikos Stangos (New York: Harper & Row, 1981), 35.

Part 2

THE WRITER

Excerpts from Kafka's
Autobiographical Writings

Kafka left behind, unintentionally to be sure, a fairly substantial body of writing that can be called autobiographical: letters, meditations on projects, notebooks, and diaries (see the Selected Bibliography). I have taken excerpts from these writings that deal first with some of Kafka's reflections on specific short stories, then with some of Kafka's thoughts about writing in general. It is to be hoped that the latter, showing how Kafka viewed his writing and the anguish that he sought to overcome, will help establish a general context for reading Kafka's fiction and finding sense in it.

[This passage, describing Kafka's experience in writing "The Judgment," is from a diary entry written in 1912.]

September 23.[1] This story, *The Judgment,* I wrote at one sitting during the night of the 22nd–23rd, from ten o'clock at night to six o'clock in the morning. I was hardly able to pull my legs out from under the desk, they had got so stiff from sitting. The fearful strain and joy, how the story developed before me, as if I were advancing over water. Several times during this night I heaved my own weight on my back. How everything can be said, how for everything, for the strangest fancies, there waits a great fire in which they perish and rise up again. How it turned blue outside the window. A wagon rolled by. Two men walked across the bridge. At two I looked at the clock for the last time. As the maid walked through the anteroom for the first time I wrote the last sentence. Turning out the light and the light of day. The slight pains around my heart. The weariness that disappeared in the middle of the night. The trembling entrance into my sisters' room. Reading aloud. Before that, stretching in the presence of the maid and saying, "I've been writing until now." The appearance of the undisturbed bed, as though it had just been brought in. The conviction verified that with my novel-writing I am in the shameful lowlands of writing. Only *in this way* can writing be done, only with such coherence, with such a complete opening out of the body and the soul. Morning in bed. The always clear eyes. Many emotions carried along in the writing, joy, for example, that I shall have something beautiful for Max's *Arkadia*, thoughts about Freud, of course; in one passage, of *Arnold Beer*; in another, of Wassermann; in one, of Werfel's giantess; of course, also of my "The Urban World."[2]

[This excerpt is from a long letter written to Felice Bauer. The "little story" refers to "The Judgment."]

[Night of 4–5 December 1912]

Oh dearest, infinitely beloved, it really is too late now for my little story, as I feared it would be; unfinished, it will lie turned heavenwards until tomorrow night; but for you, Felice, childish lady, this is the right moment, just as every moment is the right moment for you. The telegram I take as a kiss, which makes it taste good, makes for pleasure, pride, and conceit, but as a congratulation, dearest? Any other evening is more important than this one, which after all was devoted solely to my pleasure, whereas other evenings are meant for my liberation. Frankly, dearest, I simply adore reading aloud; bellowing into the audience's expectant and attentive ear warms the cockles of the poor heart. And bellow I certainly did, simply blowing away the music from adjoining rooms that was trying to spare me the trouble of reading aloud. Nothing, you know, gives the body greater satisfaction than ordering people about, or at least believing in one's ability to do so. As a child—which I was until a few years ago—I used to enjoy dreaming of reading aloud to a large, crowded hall (though equipped with somewhat greater strength of heart, voice, and intellect than I had at the time) the whole of *Éducation sentimentale* at one sitting, for as many days and nights as it required, in French of course (oh dear, my accent!), and making the walls reverberate. Whenever I have given a talk, and talking is even better than reading aloud (it's happened rarely enough), I have felt this elation, and this evening was no exception. It is—and therein lies my excuse—the only more or less public entertainment I have allowed myself in the past three months. . . . I am carrying on in a somewhat disorganized way, but if I can't do that to you, dearest, to whom else can I do it? Moreover I am sure it is all due to the reading, the remains of which still cling to my fingertips. To have something inconspicuous yet something of yours near at hand, I took along your picture postcard from the party, and decided to let my hand rest on it quite quietly during the reading, and thus—by means of the simplest magic—have your support. But as the story began to take hold of me, I began at first to play with the card, then squeezed it and bent it without thinking. Just as well the card wasn't your dear hand; had it been, you wouldn't be able to write to me tomorrow, and that would have made it far too costly an evening for me. But you don't even know your little story ["The Judgment"] yet. It is somewhat wild and mean- ingless and if it didn't express some inner truth (which can never be universally established, but has to be accepted or denied every time by each reader or listener in turn), it would be nothing. It is also hard to imagine how, being so short (seventeen typewritten pages), it could have so many faults; and I really don't know what right I have to ded- icate to you such a very doubtful creation. But we each give what we can, I the little story with myself as an appendage, you the immense gift of your love.[3]

[This excerpt from a letter to Felice offers Kafka's own evaluation of "The Judgment."]

6–7 December 1912
[Presumably during the night of 5–6 December 1912]
Cry, dearest, cry, the time for crying has come! The hero of my story died a little while ago. To comfort you, I want you to know that he died peacefully enough and reconciled to all. The story itself is still not quite finished; I am not in the right mood just now, and am leaving the end until tomorrow. Moreover, it's very late; it took me so long to recover from yesterday's disturbance.[4] It's a pity that in some passages of the story my state of exhaustion and other interruptions and extra- neous worries are so apparent; I know it could have been done more neatly; this is particularly conspicuous in the more tender passages. That is the ever-gnawing realization: in more favourable circumstances, with the creative powers I feel within me, and quite apart from their strength and endurance, I could have achieved a neater, more telling,

better-constructed piece of work than the one that now exists. This is a feeling which no amount of reasoning can dispel, though of course it is reason, too, that is right in saying that since there are no circumstances other than real ones, one cannot take any others into account, either. However that may be, I hope to finish the story tomorrow, and to return to the novel the following day.[5]

[These paragraphs are excerpted from the diaries for 1913 and again provide an insight into Kafka's opinion of his work.]

February 11. While I read the proofs of *The Judgment*, I'll write down all the relationships which have become clear to me in the story as far as I now remember them. This is necessary because the story came out of me like a real birth, covered with filth and slime, and only I have the hand that can reach to the body itself and the strength of desire to do so.

The friend is the link between father and son, he is their strongest common bond. Sitting alone at his window, Georg rummages voluptuously in this consciousness of what they have in common, believes he has his father within him, and would be at peace with everything if it were not for a fleeting, sad thoughtfulness. In the course of the story the father, with the strengthened position that the other, lesser things they share in common give him—love, devotion to the mother, loyalty to her memory, the clientele that he (the father) had been the first to acquire for the business—uses the common bond of the friend to set himself up as Georg's antagonist. Georg is left with nothing; the bride, who lives in the story only in relation to the friend, that is, to what father and son have in common, is easily driven away by the father since no marriage has yet taken place, and so she cannot penetrate the circle of blood relationship that is drawn around father and son. What they have in common is built up entirely around the father, Georg can feel it only as something foreign, something that has become independent, that he has never given enough protection, that is exposed to Russian revolutions, and only because he himself has lost everything except his awareness of the father does the judgment, which closes off his father from him completely, have so strong an effect on him.

Georg has the same number of letters as Franz. In Bendemann,

Excerpts from Kafka's Autobiographical Writings

"mann" is a strengthening of "Bende" to provide for all the as yet unforeseen possibilities in the story. But Bende has exactly the same number of letters as Kafka, and the vowel *e* occurs in the same places as does the vowel *a* in Kafka.

Frieda has as many letters as F. and the same initial, Brandenfeld has the same initial as B., and in the word "Feld" a certain connection in meaning, as well. Perhaps even the thought of Berlin was not without influence and the recollection of the Mark Brandenburg perhaps had some influence.[6]

[This letter to Felice, quoted in its entirety, also examines the use of names in "The Judgment."]

[2 June 1913]

Dearest Felice, please write and tell me about yourself, as in the old days, about the office, about your friends, your family, your walks, about books; you have no idea how important it is to my life.

Can you discover any meaning in the "Judgment"—some straightforward, coherent meaning that one could follow? I can't find any, nor can I explain anything in it. But there are a number of strange things about it. Just look at the names! It was written at a time when I had not yet written to you, though I had met you and the world had grown in value owing to your existence. Now note this. Georg has the same number of letters as Franz, "Bendemann" is made up of Bende and Mann, Bende has the same number of letters as Kafka, and the two vowels are also in the same place; out of pity for poor "Bende," "Mann" is probably meant to fortify him for his struggles. "Frieda" has the same number of letters as Felice; it also starts with the same letter: "Friede" and "Glück" are also closely related: "Brandenfeld," owing to "feld," has some connection with "Bauer," and also starts with the same letter.[7] And there are other similar things—all of which, needless to say, I only discovered afterwards. The whole thing, incidentally, was written during a single night, from eleven to six in the morning. When I sat down to write, after a Sunday so miserable I could have screamed (I had spent the entire afternoon silently circling around my brother-in-law's relatives, who were on their first visit to us), I meant to describe a war; from his window a young man was to see a vast crowd advancing across the bridge, but then the whole thing turned in my hands into something else.—And one more thing: The final word in the penultimate sentence should read "drop," not "fall." And now, is all well again?

Franz[8]

[This is a brief excerpt from a letter to Felice concerning "The Judgment."]

10 June 1913
. . . The "Judgment" cannot be explained. Perhaps one day I'll show you some entries in my diary about it. The story is full of abstractions, though they are never admitted. The friend is hardly a real person, perhaps he is more whatever the father and Georg have in common. The story may be a journey around father and son, and the friend's changing shape may be a change in perspective in the relationship between father and son. But I am not quite sure of this, either.[9]

[In this excerpt from the diaries for 1917 Kafka discusses the influence Dickens had on his work.]

[8 October 1917]
. . . Dickens's *Copperfield*. "The Stoker" a sheer imitation of Dickens, the projected novel even more so. The story of the trunk, the boy who delights and charms everyone, the menial labor, his sweetheart in the country house, the dirty houses, *et al.*, but above all the method. It was my intention, as I now see, to write a Dickens novel, but enhanced by the sharper lights I should have taken from the times and the duller ones I should have got from myself. Dickens's opulence and great, careless prodigality, but in consequence passages of awful insipidity in which he wearily works over effects he has already achieved. Gives one a barbaric impression because the whole does not make sense, a barbarism that I, it is true, thanks to my weakness and wiser for my epigonism, have been able to avoid. There is a heartlessness behind his sentimentally overflowing style. These rude characterizations which are artificially stamped on everyone and without which Dickens would

not be able to get on with his story even for a moment. (Walser resembles him in his use of vague, abstract metaphors.)[10]

[This excerpt from a letter to Felice describes Kafka's work on "The Metamorphosis."]

23 November 1912
Dearest, oh God, how I love you! It is very late at night; I have put aside my little story, on which I really haven't worked at all these last two evenings, and which is quietly developing into a much bigger story. How could I give it to you to read, even if it were finished? It is rather illegible, and even if that weren't an obstacle—up to now I certainly haven't spoiled you with beautiful writing—I don't want to send you anything to read. I want to read it to you. Yes, that would be lovely, to read this story to you, while I would have to hold your hand, for the story is a little frightening. It is called *Metamorphosis*, and it would thoroughly scare you, you might not want to hear a word of it, for alas! I scare you enough every day with my letters. . . .

I am too depressed at the moment, and perhaps I shouldn't be writing at all. But my story's hero has also had a very bad time today, and yet it is only the last lap of his misfortune, which is now becoming permanent. So how can I be particularly cheerful![11]

[This excerpt from a letter to Felice narrates Kafka's progress on "The Metamorphosis."]

24 November 1912
[Begun during the night of 23–24 November]
Dearest, once again I am putting aside this exceptionally repulsive story in order to refresh myself by thinking of you. By now it is more than half finished, and on the whole I am not too dissatisfied; but it is infinitely repulsive, and these things, you see, spring from the same heart in which you dwell and which you tolerate as a dwelling place. But don't be unhappy about it, for who knows, the more I write and the more I liberate myself, the cleaner and the worthier of you I may become, but no doubt there is a great deal more to be got rid of, and

the nights can never be long enough for this business which, incidentally, is highly voluptuous.[12]

[This reference to "The Metamorphosis" is excerpted from Kafka's diaries of 1914.]

January 19. Anxiety alternating with self-assurance at the office. Otherwise more confident. Great antipathy to "Metamorphosis." Unreadable ending. Imperfect almost to its very marrow. It would have turned out much better if I had not been interrupted at the time by the business trip.[13]

[Kafka wrote this letter to the publisher of "The Metamorphosis" concerning the illustrations planned for the story.]

To Kurt Wolff Verlag
Prague, October 25, 1915
Dear Sir,
    You recently mentioned that Ottomar Starke[14] is going to do a drawing for the title page of *Metamorphosis*. Insofar as I know the artist's style from *Napoleon*, this prospect has given me a minor and perhaps unnecessary fright. It struck me that Starke, as an illustrator, might want to draw the insect itself. Not that, please not that! I do not want to restrict him, but only to make this plea out of my deeper knowledge of the story. The insect itself cannot be depicted. It cannot even be shown from a distance. Perhaps there is no such intention and my plea can be dismissed with a smile—so much the better. But I would be very grateful if you would pass along my request and make it more emphatic. If I were to offer suggestions for an illustration, I would choose such scenes as the following: the parents and the head clerk in front of the locked door, or even better, the parents and the sister in the lighted room, with the door open upon the adjoining room that lies in darkness.[15]
    I imagine you have already received the proofs and the reviews.
                    With best regards, sincerely yours, Franz Kafka[16]

Excerpts from Kafka's Autobiographical Writings

[This passage is excerpted from *Conversations with Kafka*, the notes and reminiscences of Kafka's friend, Gustav Janouch. In this particular conversation Janouch is visiting a bed-ridden Kafka in order to show him a copy of *Lady into Fox*, a book by an English author, David Garnett, which a student named Bachrach had lent to Janouch. Bachrach had commented that Kafka was becoming world famous since the English writer's book was a copy of "The Metamorphosis."]

. . . I took the English book out of my pocket, laid it on the counterpane in front of Kafka, and told him about my latest conversation with Bachrach. When I said that Garnett's book imitated the method of *The Metamorphosis*, he gave a tired smile, and with a faint dissenting movement of his head said: "But no! He didn't get that from me. It's a matter of the age. We both copied from that. Animals are closer to us than human beings. That's where our prison bars lie. We find relations with animals easier than with men." . . .

The following week he was not at the office. It was ten days or a fortnight before I was able to walk home with him. He gave me the book and said: "Every man lives behind bars, which he carries within him. That is why people write so much about animals now. It's an expression of longing for a free natural life. But for human beings the natural life is a human life. But men don't always realize that. They refuse to realize it. Human existence is a burden to them, so they dispose of it in fantasies."[17]

[The subject of this conversation between Kafka and Janouch, quoted in its entirety, is once again "The Metamorphosis."]

My friend Alfred Kämpf from Altsattel near Falkenau, whose acquaintance I had made in Elbogen, admired Kafka's story *The Metamorphosis*. He described the author as "a new, more profound and therefore more significant Edgar Allan Poe."

During a walk with Franz Kafka on the Altstädter Ring I told him about this new admirer of his, but aroused neither interest nor understanding. On the contrary, Kafka's expression showed that any discussion of his book was distasteful to him. I, however, was filled with a zeal for discoveries, and so I was tactless.

"The hero of the story is called Samsa," I said. "It sounds like a cryptogram for Kafka. Five letters in each word. The S in the word Samsa has the same position as the K in the word Kafka. The A. . ."

Kafka interrupted me.

"It is not a cryptogram. Samsa is not merely Kafka, and nothing else. _The Metamorphosis_ is not a confession, although it is—in a certain sense—an indiscretion."

"I know nothing about that."

"Is it perhaps delicate and discreet to talk about the bugs in one's own family?"

"It isn't usual in good society."

"You see what bad manners I have."

Kafka smiled. He wished to dismiss the subject. But I did not wish to.

"It seems to me that the distinction between good and bad manners hardly applies here," I said. "_The Metamorphosis_ is a terrible dream, a terrible conception."

Kafka stood still.

"The dream reveals the reality, which conception lags behind. That is the horror of life—the terror of art. But now I must go home."

He took a curt farewell.

Had I driven him away?

I felt ashamed.[18]

[In this letter to his publisher, Kafka offers, in a roundabout manner, some insights on "The Judgment" and "In the Penal Colony."]

To Kurt Wolff Verlag
[Prague, 19 August 1916]
Dear Sirs,

In reply to your kind letter of the 15th, let me sum up the reasons for my request that "The Judgment" and "In the Penal Colony" be published as individual volumes.

Initially there was no talk of issuing them in _Der jüngste Tag_ series, but only of a volume of stories, _Punishments_ (containing "The Judgment"—"Metamorphosis"—"In the Penal Colony"), which Herr Wolff projected a long while ago. These stories have a certain unity and as a group would naturally have bulked up to a more substantial volume than any of the numbers of _Der jüngste Tag_. Nevertheless I would gladly give up the book if I saw the possibility that "The Judgment" could be issued as a separate work.

The question is hardly whether to publish "The Judgment" and "In the Penal Colony" together as a *Jüngste Tag* book, for "In the Penal Colony" is quite long enough, as you yourself have estimated in your last letter, to suffice for a volume of its own. I only wish to add that to my mind "The Judgment" and "In the Penal Colony" would make a dreadful combination; "Metamorphosis" might still mediate between them, but without that story you would have two alien heads knocking violently at each other.

May I cite the following special arguments for publishing "The Judgment" by itself. The story is more poetic than narrative and therefore needs open space around it if it is to exert its force. It is also my favorite work and so I always wished for it to be appreciated if possible by itself. Since the idea of the volume of stories has been dropped, now would be the best opportunity for this. Incidentally—if "In the Penal Colony" were not to appear right off in *Der jüngste Tag*, I would be able to offer it to the *Weissen Blätter*. But that is really only incidental, for my principal concern remains that "The Judgment" be published by itself.[19]

[This conversation between Kafka and Gustav Janouch, quoted in its entirety, focuses on Kafka's feelings about the publication of his work; in this particular instance, "In the Penal Colony."]

I had called on Franz Kafka in his office at the very moment when a proof copy of his story, *In the Penal Settlement*, arrived by post. Kafka opened the grey wrapper, without knowing what it contained. But when he opened the green-and-black bound volume and recognized his work, he was obviously embarrassed.

He opened the drawer of his desk, looked at me, closed the drawer, and handed me the book.

"You will certainly want to see the book."

I answered with a smile, opened the volume, gave a hurried look at the printing and paper and gave him the book back, as I realized his nervousness.

"It is beautifully done," I said. "A really representative Drugulin Press production. You should be very satisfied, Herr Doktor."

The Writer

"That I really am not," said Franz Kafka, and pushed the book care-lessly into a drawer, which he closed. "Publication of some scribble of mine always upsets me."

"Then why do you allow it to be printed?"

"That's just it! Max Brod, Felix Weltsch,[20] all my friends always take possession of something I have written and then take me by surprise with a completed contract with the publisher. I do not want to cause them any unpleasantness, and so it all ends in the publication of things which are entirely personal notes or diversions. Personal proofs of my human weakness are printed, and even sold, because my friends, with Max Brod at their head, have conceived the idea of making literature out of them, and because I have not the strength to destroy this evi-dence of solitude."

After a short pause he said in a different voice:

"What I have just said is, of course, an exaggeration, and a piece of malice against my friends. In fact, I am so corrupt and shameless that I myself co-operate in publishing these things. As an excuse for my own weakness, I make circumstances stronger than they really are. That, of course, is a piece of deceit. But after all, I am a lawyer. So I can never get away from evil."[21]

[This passage is excerpted from Kafka's diaries for 1914. This entry contains not only a reference to "The Village Schoolmaster," but also a comment on the process of beginning a story.]

December 19. Yesterday wrote "The Village Schoolmaster" almost without knowing it, but was afraid to go on later than a quarter to two; the fear was well founded. I slept hardly at all, merely suffered through perhaps three short dreams and was then in the office in the condition one would expect. Yesterday Father's reproaches on account of the factory: "You talked me into it." Then went home and calmly wrote for three hours in the consciousness that my guilt is beyond question, though not so great as Father pictures it. Today, Saturday, did not come to dinner, partly in fear of Father, partly in order to use the whole night for working; yet I wrote only one page that wasn't very good.

The beginning of every story is ridiculous at first. There seems no hope that this newborn thing, still incomplete and tender in every joint, will be able to keep alive in the completed organization of the world, which, like every completed organization, strives to close itself off. However, one should not forget that the story, if it has any justification to exist, bears its complete organization within itself even before it has been fully formed; for this reason despair over the beginning of a story is unwarranted; in a like case parents should have to despair of their suckling infant, for they had no intention of bringing this pathetic and ridiculous being into the world. Of course, one never knows whether the despair one feels is warranted or unwarranted. But reflecting on it can give one a certain support; in the past I have suffered from the lack of this knowledge.[22]

[This excerpt from a diary entry for 1914 reflects the difficulty Kafka often experienced in writing.]

December 26. In Kuttenberg with Max and his wife. How I counted on the four free days, how many hours I pondered how best to spend them, and now perhaps disappointed after all. Tonight wrote almost nothing and am in all likelihood no longer capable of going on with "The Village Schoolmaster," which I have been working at for a week now, and which I should certainly have completed in three free nights, perfect and with no external defect; but now, in spite of the fact that I am still virtually at the beginning, it already has two irremediable defects and in addition is stunted.—New schedule from now on! Use the time even better![23]

[The remaining excerpts from Kafka's letters and diaries deal with his attitude toward writing in general. This first one is from a letter written to Oskar Pollak, Kafka's friend and schoolmate.]

[Prague, November 9, 1903]
Dear Oskar,
. . . By the way, no writing's been done for some time. It's this way with me: God doesn't want me to write, but I—I must. So there's an everlasting up and down; after all, God is the stronger, and there's

more anguish in it than you can imagine. So many powers within me are tied to a stake, which might possibly grow into a green tree. Released, they could be useful to me and the country. But nobody ever shook a millstone from around his neck by complaining, especially when he was fond of it.[24]

[This excerpt is from Kafka's diaries for 1910. The "story" referred to remains unidentified.]

10 o'clock, November 15. I will not let myself become tired. I'll jump into my story even though it should cut my face to pieces.[25]

[This excerpt is from Kafka's diaries for 1910.]

December 15. I simply do not believe the conclusions I have drawn from my present condition, which has already lasted almost a year, my condition is too serious for that. Indeed, I do not even know whether I can say that it is not a new condition. My real opinion, however, is that this condition is new—I have had similar ones, but never one like this. It is as if I were made of stone, as if I were my own tombstone, there is no loophole for doubt or for faith, for love or repugnance, for courage or anxiety, in particular or in general, only a vague hope lives on, but no better than the inscriptions on tombstones. Almost every word I write jars against the next, I hear the consonants rub leadenly against each other and the vowels sing an accompaniment like Negroes in a minstrel show. My doubts stand in a circle around every word, I see them before I see the word, but what then! I do not see the word at all, I invent it. Of course, that wouldn't be the greatest misfortune, only I ought to be able to invent words capable of blowing the odor of corpses in a direction other than straight into mine and the reader's face. When I sit down at the desk I feel no better than someone who falls and breaks both legs in the middle of the traffic of the Place de l'Opéra. All the carriages, despite their noise, press silently from all directions in all directions, but that man's pain keeps better order than the police, it closes his eyes and empties the Place and the streets without the carriages having to turn about. The great commotion hurts him, for he is really an obstruction to traffic, but the emptiness is no less sad, for it unshackles his real pain.[26]

[This entry, quoted in its entirety, is from the diaries for 1911 and immediately follows an entry dated 27 December.]

My feeling when I write something that is wrong might be depicted as follows: In front of two holes in the ground a man is waiting for something to appear that can rise up only out of the hole on his right. But while this hole remains covered over by a dimly visible lid, one thing after another rises up out of the hole on his left, keeps trying to attract his attention, and in the end succeeds in doing this without any difficulty because of its swelling size, which, much as the man may try to prevent it, finally covers up even the right hole. But the man—he does not want to leave this place, and indeed refuses to at any price—has nothing but these appearances, and although—fleeting as they are, their strength is used up by their merely appearing—they cannot satisfy him, he still strives, whenever out of weakness they are arrested in their rising up, to drive them up and scatter them into the air if only he can thus bring up others; for the permanent sight of one is unbearable, and moreover he continues to hope that after the false appearances have been exhausted, the true will finally appear.

How weak this picture is. An incoherent assumption is thrust like a board between the actual feeling and the metaphor of the description.[27]

[The "little book" mentioned in this entry from the diaries of 1912 refers to Kafka's collection of stories entitled *Meditation*.]

August 11. Nothing, nothing. How much time the publishing of the little book takes from me and how much harmful, ridiculous pride comes from reading old things with an eye to publication. Only that keeps me from writing. And yet in reality I have achieved nothing, the disturbance is the best proof of it. In any event, now, after the publication of the book, I will have to stay away from magazines and reviews even more than before, if I do not wish to be content with just sticking the tips of my fingers into the truth. How immovable I have become!

The Writer

Formerly, if I said only one word that opposed the direction of the moment, I at once flew over to the other side, now I simply look at myself and remain as I am.[28]

[These three letters were all written to Felice Bauer.]

From 23 to 24 December 1912
Dearest, what will happen when I cannot write any more? This moment seems to have arrived; for a week or more I have accomplished nothing; in the course of the last ten nights (admittedly working with frequent interruptions) I was really carried away only once, that was all. I am permanently tired, my craving for sleep goes around and around in my head. Tension right and left at the top of my skull. Yesterday I began a little story which I had very much at heart and which appeared to open up before me at one stroke;[29] today it is completely closed up; when I ask what will happen, I am not thinking of myself, I have lived through worse times, and am still more or less alive, and if I am not going to write for myself, I shall have more time to write to you, to enjoy the nearness of you, this nearness which I have created by thinking, by writing, and by fighting with all the strength of my soul—but you, you will not be able to love me any more. Not because I am not going to write for myself any more, but because this not writing will turn me into a poorer, more unbalanced, less secure being, whom you could not possibly like. Dearest, if you make poor children in the street happy, do it to me too, I am no less poor; you have no idea how great my affinity is with the old man who goes home in the evening with his unsold wares—so do unto me as you would to all of them, even if your mother should be angry about this as she was about the others (everyone has to bear his burden unconditionally; for parents it is the anger over their children's innocent nature): in short, tell me you will go on loving me, no matter how I behave go on loving me at any price, there is no disgrace I would not be prepared to bear—but where is this leading me?[30]

From 14 to 15 January 1913
Dearest, while I have been writing it has got very late again. At around two o'clock every morning I keep remembering the Chinese scholar.

Excerpts from Kafka's Autobiographical Writings

Alas, it is not my mistress who calls me, it's only the letter I want to write to her. You once said you would like to sit beside me while I write. Listen, in that case I could not write (I can't do much, anyway), but in that case I could not write at all. For writing means revealing oneself to excess; that utmost of self-revelation and surrender, in which a human being, when involved with others, would feel he was losing himself, and from which, therefore, he will always shrink as long as he is in his right mind—for everyone wants to live as long as he is alive—even the degree of self-revelation and surrender is not enough for writing. Writing that springs from the surface of existence—when there is no other way and the deeper wells have dried up—is nothing, and collapses the moment a truer emotion makes that surface shake. This is why one can never be alone enough when one writes, why there can never be enough silence around one when one writes, why even night is not night enough. This is why there is never enough time at one's disposal, for the roads are long and it is easy to go astray, there are even times when one becomes afraid and has the desire—even without any constraint or enticement—to run back (a desire always severely punished later on), how much more so if one were suddenly to receive a kiss from the most beloved lips! I have often thought that the best mode of life for me would be to sit in the innermost room of a spacious locked cellar with my writing things and a lamp. Food would be brought and always put down far away from my room, outside the cellar's outermost door. The walk to my food, in my dressing gown, through the vaulted cellars, would be my only exercise. I would then return to my table, eat slowly and with deliberation, then start writing again at once. And how I would write! From what depths I would drag it up! Without effort! For extreme concentration knows no effort. The trouble is that I might not be able to keep it up for long, and at the first failure—which perhaps even in these circumstances could not be avoided—would be bound to end in a grandiose fit of madness. *What do you think, dearest? Don't be reticent with your cellar-dweller.*

Franz[31]

26 June 1913

. . . My attitude to my writing and my attitude to people is unchangeable; it is a part of my nature, and not due to temporary circumstances. What I need for my writing is seclusion, not "like a hermit," that would not be enough, but like the dead. Writing, in this sense, is a sleep deeper than that of death, and just as one would not and cannot tear the dead from their graves, so I must not and cannot be torn from my desk at night. This has no immediate bearing on my relationship with people; it is simply that I can write only in this regular, continuous, and rigorous fashion, and therefore can live only in this way too. But as you say, for you it will be "rather difficult." I have always had this fear of people, not actually of the people themselves, but of their intrusion upon my weak nature; for even the most intimate friend to set foot in my room fills me with terror, and is more than just a symbol of this fear.[32]

[This excerpt is from the diaries for 1915.]

February 9. Wrote a little today and yesterday. Dog story.[33]

Just now read the beginning. It is ugly and gives me a headache. In spite of all its truth it is wicked, pedantic, mechanical, a fish barely breathing on a sandbank. I write my *Bouvard et Pécuchet* prematurely. If the two elements—most pronounced in "The Stoker" and "In the Penal Colony"—do not combine, I am finished. But is there any prospect of their combining?[34]

[In this letter to Milena Jesenská, Kafka discusses his deep feelings of fear and anxiety.]

[July 15, 1920]

One can get certain results, after all, if one only has the courage:

Firstly, perhaps Gross[35] is not so wrong, so far as I understand him; at least it speaks for him that I'm still alive, though according to the special distribution of my inner forces should actually be dead long ago.

Secondly, how things will develop later is not the question, all that's certain is that *away from you I can't live otherwise than by giving in completely to fear, giving in more than it asks, and I do so without compulsion, with rapture, I pour myself into it.*

You're right for reproaching me in the name of fear for my behaviour in Vienna, but in this respect fear is really mysterious, I don't know its inner laws, I know only its hand at my throat, and this is really *the most terrible thing I've ever experienced or could experience.*

It follows, perhaps, that we are now both married, you in Vienna, I to my Fear in Prague, and that not only you, but I too, tug in vain at our marriage. For, look, Milena, if in Vienna you had been *completely convinced* by me (agreeing even with that step the wisdom of which you doubted), you would no longer be in Vienna in spite of everything, or rather there would be no "in spite of everything," you would simply be in Prague and everything by which you console yourself in your last letter is after all simply consolation. Don't you think so?

Had you come to Prague at once, or at least decided in its favour at once, it would not actually have been a proof for you, I don't need any proofs for you, you are beyond everything clear and safe to me, but it would have been a great proof for myself, and this I now lack. On this, too, Fear occasionally feeds. Indeed it is perhaps even worse, and just I, the "Saviour," am detaining you in Vienna as no one else has yet.[36]

[This entry is from the diaries in 1922 and further describes Kafka's feeling of angst.]

January 16. This past week I suffered something very like a breakdown; the only one to match it was on that night two years ago; apart from then I have never experienced its like. Everything seemed over with, even today there is no great improvement to be noticed. One can put two interpretations on the breakdown, both of which are probably correct.

First: breakdown, impossible to sleep, impossible to stay awake, impossible to endure life, or, more exactly, the course of life. The clocks are not in unison; the inner one runs crazily on at a devilish or demoniac or in any case inhuman pace, the outer one limps along at its usual speed. What else can happen but that the two worlds split apart, and they do split apart, or at least clash in a fearful manner. There are doubtless several reasons for the wild tempo of the inner process; the most obvious one is introspection, which will suffer no idea to sink tranquilly to rest but must pursue each one into consciousness, only itself to become an idea, in turn to be pursued by renewed introspection.

Second: This pursuit, originating in the midst of men, carries one in a direction away from them. The solitude that for the most part has been forced on me, in part voluntarily sought by me—but what was this if not compulsion too?—is now losing all its ambiguity and approaches its dénouement. Where is it leading? The strongest likelihood is, that it may lead to madness; there is nothing more to say, the pursuit goes right through me and rends me asunder. Or I can—can I?—manage to keep my feet somewhat and be carried along in the wild pursuit. Where, then, shall I be brought? "Pursuit," indeed, is only a metaphor. I can also say, "assault on the last earthly frontier," an assault, moreover, launched from below, from mankind, and since this too is a metaphor, I can replace it by the metaphor of an assault from above, aimed at me from above.

All such writing is an assault on the frontiers; if Zionism had not intervened, it might easily have developed into a new secret doctrine, a Kabbalah. There are intimations of this. Though of course it would require genius of an unimaginable kind to strike root again in the old centuries, or create the old centuries anew and not spend itself withal, but only then begin to flower forth.[37]

[This is an excerpt from a letter to Max Brod, Kafka's lifelong friend, companion, and biographer.]

[Planá; postmark: July 5, 1922]
. . . Last night as I lay sleepless and let everything continually veer back and forth between my aching temples, what I had almost forgotten during the last relatively quiet time became clear to me: namely, on what frail ground or rather altogether nonexistent ground I live, over a darkness from which the dark power emerges when it wills and, heedless of my stammering, destroys my life. Writing sustains me, but is it not more accurate to say that it sustains this kind of life? By this I don't mean, of course, that my life is better when I don't write. Rather it is much worse then and wholly unbearable and has to end in madness. But that, granted, only follows from the postulate that I am a writer, which is actually true even when I am not writing, and a nonwriting writer is a monster inviting madness. But what about being a writer itself? Writing is a sweet and wonderful reward, but for what? In the night it became clear to me, as clear as a child's lesson book, that

it is the reward for serving the devil. This descent to the dark powers, this unshackling of spirits bound by nature, these dubious embraces and whatever else may take place in the nether parts which the higher parts no longer know, when one writes one's stories in the sunshine. Perhaps there are other forms of writing, but I know only this kind; at night, when fear keeps me from sleeping, I know only this kind. And the diabolic element in it seems very clear to me. It is vanity and sensuality which continually buzz about one's own or even another's form—and feast on him. The movement multiples itself—it is a regular solar system of vanity. Sometimes a naïve person will wish, "I would like to be dead and see how everyone mourns me." Such a writer is continually staging such a scene: He dies (or rather he does not live) and continually mourns himself. From this springs a terrible fear of death, which need not reveal itself as fear of death but may also appear as fear of change, as fear of Georgental. The reasons for this fear of death may be divided into two main categories. First he has a terrible fear of dying because he has not yet lived. By this I do not mean that wife and child, fields and cattle are essential to living. What is essential to life is only to forgo complacency, to move into the house instead of admiring it and hanging garlands around it. In reply to this, one might say that this is a matter of fate and is not given into anyone's hand. But then why this sense of repining, this repining that never ceases? To make oneself finer and more savory? That is a part of it. But why do such nights leave one always with the refrain: I could live and I do not live. The second reason—perhaps it is all really one, the two do not want to stay apart for me now—is the belief: "What I have play-acted is really going to happen. I have not bought myself off by my writing. I died my whole life long and now I will really die. My life was sweeter than other peoples' and my death will be more terrible by the same degree. Of course the writer in me will die right away, since such a figure has no base, no substance, is less than dust. He is only barely possible in the broil of earthly life, is only a construct of sensuality. That is your writer for you. But I myself cannot go on living because I have not lived, I have remained clay, I have not blown the spark into fire, but only used it to light up my corpse." It will be a strange burial: the writer, insubstantial as he is, consigning the old corpse, the longtime corpse, to the grave. I am enough of a writer to appreciate the scene with all my senses, or—and it is the same thing—to want to describe it with total self-forgetfulnesss—not alertness, but self-forgetfulness is the writer's first prerequisite. But there will be no more of such describing. But why am I talking of actual dying? It is just the same in life. I sit here in the comfortable posture of the writer, ready for all sorts of fine things, and must idly look on—for what can I do but write?—as my true ego, this wretched, defenseless ego, is nipped by the devil's pincers, cudgeled, and almost ground to pieces on a random pretext—a little trip to Georgental. . . . The existence of a writer is an argument against the existence of the soul, for the soul has obviously taken flight from the real ego, but not improved itself, only become a writer.[38]

[This last excerpt is from a letter to Max Brod.]

[Planá; postmark: July 12, 1922]
. . . And the writing? (This is going ahead here, less than average in quality, no more, and constantly endangered by noise.) Possibly my explanation will not make sense to you and only comes down to the fact that I want to have your writing as close as possible to mine. And certainly there is this difference, that I, should I ever have been happy, outside of writing and whatever is connected with it (I don't rightly know if I ever was)—at such times I was incapable of writing, with the result that everything had barely begun when the whole applecart tipped over, for the longing to write was always uppermost. This does not mean that I am fundamentally, innately, and honorably a writer by nature. I am away from home and must always write home, even if any home of mine has long since floated away into eternity. All this writing is nothing but Robinson Crusoe's flag hoisted at the highest point of the island.[39]

Notes

1. This entry is preceded by the complete draft of *The Judgment*.

2. *The Diaries of Franz Kafka, 1910 to 1913*, trans. Joseph Kresh, ed. Max Brod (New York: Schocken Books, 1976), 275–76.

3. *Letters to Felice*, trans. James Stern and Elizabeth Duckworth, ed. Erich Heller and Jürgen Born (Harmondsworth, N.Y.: Penguin Books, 1978), 195–96.

4. Presumably the public reading of Prague authors on 4 December.

5. *Letters to Felice*, 199.

6. *Diaries, 1910 to 1913*, 278–79.

7. *Friede* = peace, *Glück* = happiness (Latin: *felicitas*), *Feld* = field, and *Bauer* = peasant.

8. *Letters to Felice*, 382–83.

9. Ibid., 384–85.

10. *The Diaries of Franz Kafka, 1914 to 1923*, trans. Joseph Kresh, ed. Max Brod (New York: Schocken Books, 1976), 188–89.

11. *Letters to Felice*, 164.

12. Ibid., 165.

13. *Diaries, 1914 to 1923*, 12.

14. Ottomar Starke (1886–1962), stage designer and illustrator, created many covers and illustrations for *Jüngste Tag* series.

15. Starke's design on the cover of the published book shows in the background, a folding door with one wing ajar, and the left foreground a man in a morning coat, hands clasped to his face.

16. *Letters to Friends, Family and Editors*, trans. Richard Winston and Clara Winston (New York: Schocken Books, 1977), 114–15.

17. Gustav Janouch, *Conversations with Kafka*, trans. Gorowny Rees, 2nd ed. (New York: New Directions Books, 1971), 22–23.

18. *Conversations with Kafka*, 31–32.

19. *Letters to Friends, Family and Editors*, 125–26.

20. Felix Weltsch (1884–1964), philosopher and publicist was editor-in-chief of the Prague Zionist weekly, *Selbstwehr* (Self-Defence).

21. *Conversations with Kafka*, 25–26.

22. *Diaries, 1914 to 1923*, 103–4.

23. Ibid., 105.

24. *Letters to Friends, Family and Editors*, 10.

25. *Diaries, 1910 to 1913*, 31.

26. Ibid., 32–33.

27. Ibid., 200–201.

28. Ibid., 266.

29. The fragment of this story seems not to have been preserved.

30. *Letters to Felice*, 234.

31. Ibid., 271–72.

32. Ibid., 399.

33. Not the "Investigations of a Dog" in *The Great Wall of China*.

34. *Diaries, 1914 to 1923*, 114–15.

35. Otto Gross, the Viennese psychoanalyst and philosopher.

36. *Letters to Milena*, trans. Tania and James Stern, ed. Willi Haas (New York: Schocken Books, 1981), 106–7.

37. *Diaries, 1914 to 1923*, 201–3.

38. *Letters to Friends, Family and Editors*, 333–34.

39. Ibid., 339–40.

Part 3

THE CRITICS

The purpose of this section is to illustrate briefly different types of critical responses to Kafka's short stories. The first essay by Stanley Corngold is a useful introduction to the problems posed by the rhetoric of Kafka's fiction. Following are excerpts from critical essays illustrating a feminist viewpoint by Ruth V. Gross, a theological interpretation by Doreen F. Fowler, a Freudian reading by William J. Dodd, and finally a Marxist approach by Walter H. Sokel. These critical texts are representative of the wealth of critical reactions that Kafka's fiction can generate, and I hope that they will encourage readers to pursue their own interpretations.

Kafka's Narrative Perspective

*Stanley Corngold**

In the beginning, the world was a simple place, and Kafka was admired for the simplicity of his narration. This was a long time ago, before the discovery of *erlebte Rede* (narrated monologue) and *Einsinnigkeit* (congruence or monopolized perspective). It then seemed possible to say without much ado what Kafka meant. But the growing sense of the shakiness of even the most convinced readings raised a general doubt. The conscientious interpreter decided to say, with respect to Kafka: "I am a person of no convictions—at least I think I'm not." Such irony is at any rate more faithful to Kafka than the counter-transference of the hysterical reader who, unpleasantly exercised by the hermeneutic lure of a work that "invites rape but resists penetration," declares it finally without meaning.

I want to describe this progress from certainty to uncertainty in Kafka-interpretation on the axis of our understanding of Kafka's narrative perspective.

In the beginning it was assumed of Kafka's novels (and of the stories written between 1912 and 1914) that by virtue of the third-person hero and the preterite tense, the subject matter was being narrated from an objective, authoritative standpoint. The text could be read as embodying the intention of the author (Kafka) whose privileged representative was the narrator. Consciousness in the novel (all perceiving and valuing) was then divided essentially between the narrator and the hero. The hero a deluded but cautionary example; the narrator lucid, holding up the character's blindness to our judgment.

Beissner's important work in 1952 developed the opposite notion of *Einsinnigkeit*. Now, it appeared that the perspective of many of Kafka's works never exceeded that of the hero, was only as knowing and as ignorant as the hero, anchored to his very place in space and time. As a result it became impossible to divide consciousness in the work between higher and lower, deluded and clear. Consciousness was uniform—and rather opaque; the mood of Kafka's novels was that of his

*Reprinted by permission from the *Newsletter of the Kafka Society of America* 1 (June 1978):8–10.

Stanley Corngold

heroes, a sort of harassed perplexity. *Their* consciousness attuned the work—circular, repetitive and bewildered, their projects forever only duplicating their obsessive ideas. This impression of evasiveness was one which it was impossible to dispel by an appeal to the narrator—there allegedly being none. Such a situation of course entails what is nowadays called the undecidability of the work. From inside a consciousness that grasps the world immediately, not critically—for which the world is sheer evidence, givenness, in its just being-there—it's impossible to undertake a critique either of this consciousness or of the world. The reader can reject either one or both; but his judgment is then founded on feelings and beliefs which the novels don't share.

But undecidability is almost always intolerable; and it is therefore only a little ironical that Beissner, the discoverer of the congruent perspective, had no intention whatsoever of abiding with undecidability, of holding to the unsettling, indeed insulting situation implied by his narratological discovery of the impossibility of interpretation—Kafka's epic, in Lukács' phrase, being one of "insulted and defeated spirituality." Beissner sought a solid position just marginally outside the text, appealing, in the case of "The Metamorphosis," to a cover-drawing made for the first edition, possibly with Kafka's approval—a cover-drawing which, according to Beissner, shows a young, vigorous Gregor Samsa averting his gaze from the blackness of his room and the nightmare harbored there. Thus Beissner declared Gregor's awareness of the world to be only the passing experience of a terrible hallucination. The dreadful implications of metamorphosis could be even further attenuated by the assumption that Gregor, safely recovered from his ordeal, was now narrating the horror, not indeed in the epic preterite but in the imperfect.

To keep faith with Kafka the ironist would require us to prefer now and shore up Beissner's theoretical perspective (as opposed to his practical findings), were it not for the wealth of new discoveries made by scrupulous close readers—disrupting the alleged congruence and focusing in effect on breaks in the perspective. Breaks exist between the planes of consciousness of narrator and figure. Here's one such unrecognized instance from "The Metamorphosis." Gregor is described as struggling to turn the key of the lock in his room with his jaws, "in der Vorstellung, dass . . ." ("in the delusion that . . . they [the family] were all following his efforts with suspense"). If the perspective is indeed that of immediacy, the fiction that of naiveté, it is not possible to register the experience of a delusion. The consciousness of error can come only in retrospect; but *Einsinnigkeit* really rests, of course, not so

127

much on the fusion of "viewpoint" of narrator and hero (if indeed such a thing could be conceived) as on the convention of simultaneity: the event may not be depicted as known in advance of its befalling the character. Such a moment of transgression stands for a good many throughout Kafka's works; the planes of perception and of reflective-interpretation momentarily cross.

The discovery of such breaks takes us, I think, to a point of ultimate difficulty in our understanding of Kafka's narrative perspective. The existence of such breaks appears to precipitate within the text the traces of a superior narrator—traces which, while disrupting the illusion of congruence, also inspire, by the conventions of reading, belief in the existence of an author within the text—a logician of the logic of the breaks, holding out to us the promise of authoritative meaning. Can it be that when we have once charted the pattern of his intrusions, the old expectation of the omniscient narrator will after all be fulfilled, requiring of us only that to hear him we exercise more than usual subtlety?

The trouble is that however subtly examined, these breaks have not yet fallen into an intelligible pattern; and given the fact that the novels are unfinished, they are never likely to do so. But the problem—as we shall see—isn't only an empirical one.

We frequently do not know what the specific importance is of the propositions that are immediately conveyed in another perspective; of the fact that they occur where they do; and that they stand in such or such a relation of disparity with the voice of the perspectival figure. What we can say now, unarguably (given the state of our understanding), is that they have a random character. We have been returned to undecidability of a different order.

All breaks in perspective are surprising, but not all breaks are surprising to the same degree. Whether they suddenly distance us from the hero or involve us more deeply in his fate, they may turn upside down the reading which our inexpungable tendency to interpret has been persistently elaborating, or they may suddenly seem to confirm it. In the light of the kinds of concern we bring to our reading, not all breaks will seem equally random or arbitrary: as readers we have a vested interest in diminishing their strangeness.

Even randomness can be recuperated: breaks in form can be redoubled as dramatized textual figures and acts. Such a figure is the vermin Gregor Samsa, who, it can be shown, functions in *The Metamorphosis* as a figure for pure narration and whose body throughout the story is randomly perforated. Other kinds of disruption can be recuperated as the inevitable exigencies of realistic narrative; others might provably be mistakes: "Kafka nodded."

But there are limits to this recovery of meaning. Much the most interesting class of disruptions—and the ones I mean to call attention to at this (final) juncture—are those which Kafka deliberately—or arbitrarily—included as arbitrary violations of congruence.

This class of disruptions points to an ultimate undecidability: of whether Kafka means to be undecidable or not, whether the fiction is or is not controlled by a superior narrator who *decides* when to suspend congruence and when not to.

This being the case we are so far forced to the hypothesis that in at least one vital sector Kafka's works are not the uniform product of a controlling subjectivity or intention but the disruptive outcome of an impersonal linguistic principle of irony. The narrator of Kafka's fiction is an irony that is not just a controlled trope—its meaning is neither recoverable nor stable nor finite. We glimpse here, however unsettling the idea, the expropriation of the subject Kafka in an impersonal linguistic exchange. The fact that Kafka may have collaborated in this process of self-alienation can be related to the thematics of impersonality in Kafka's autobiographical account of his writing and to the whole aleatory strain of modern aesthetics.

It would still be helpful to have a systematic empirical tabulation of the features of Kafka's breaks at the level of signifier and signified, even though the question posed here—because it puts the very possibility of a uniformity in Kafka into question—can never be a sheerly empirical one.

Of Mice and Women: Reflections on a Discourse in Kafka's "Josefine, die Sängerin oder Das Volk der Mäuse"

*Ruth V. Gross**

In dealing with the short fiction in recent years, I have noted a peculiarity, one that has been often overlooked by critics, perhaps because

*Excerpted from *The Germanic Review* 60, no. 2 (Spring 1985):59–68. Reprinted by permission of the Helen Dwight Reid Educational Foundation. © 1985.

of its obviousness. Among the overwhelming number of protagonists that are male in Kafka stories, there are also two females: one is a bridge who bears traffic, the other is a mouse who sings. Perusing these two tales can add to the current discussion of Kafka and women and provide perhaps yet another feminist approach to Kafka which may throw a different light on some of the feminist questions and provide a different sort of answer. . . .

The first paragraph of "Josephine the Singer or the Mouse Folk" sets the tone for the whole story. It contains the entire plot, such as it is, within it. It is like an overture with all the tunes of the work already included or alluded to, or like an introduction to a song, presenting the main melody. It has six sentences, all of which are negated or contain negations with the exception of the opening sentence—"Our singer is called Josephine."[1] Within the negative tone of the paragraph are couched three positive statements: (1) Josefine is the name of "our singer"; (2) the mousepeople have a certain practical slyness; and (3) Josefine loves music. This is not much of a plot, but it could sum up what the narrator goes on about for the length of the narration. Even Josefine's final disappearance is prepared for and alluded to in the last sentence of this first paragraph—"when she dies, music—who knows for how long—will vanish from our lives" (360). Like so much of Kafka's short fiction, this tale is not long on plot. The impact lies in the telling.

Josefine—the name defines her being, her essence. It is the feminine form of Joseph, Kafka's protagonist in "The Trial." In other words, it is Joseph with an appendage, a tail, if you will—a something extra that makes her feminine. Although the something extra usually defines the male, with mice it is different. The appendage-tail turns her from a man named Joseph into a female mouse. Of course, Joseph was also a patriarch of the Hebrews. As Moses led the Exodus out, Joseph led the Eisodus in before him. If, as Brod and other critics have suggested, the mousepeople are the people of Moses, the "ine," the supplement, the tail, could be seen as being caught between the two biblical patriarchs Joseph and Moses. The title, as Kafka finally revised it—"Josephine the Singer or the Mouse Folk"—reflects this. It is this name—Josefine—that lets the readers know that the singer of note here is female. The text portrays the mousepeople as a patriarchal society. Their attitude toward Josefine is paternal. In this society she, most of all, is the different one. She stands out, not only by virtue of her name, but because of her actions. As they patronize her, protect her, keep her in line, i.e., *father* her, she believes that by bringing them together, she protects them, saves them, gives them strength, dominates them, i.e., *mothers* them. The name becomes the semantic indicator of difference—that which makes Josefine Josefine—the other, the mother of her people. . . .

Josefine, . . . has no defenses, and her name, as we have seen, is merely a patriarchal trope. She is not more, not less than her song. When she sings, she sings herself: When she ceases to sing, she must herself disappear. But in her song, the song that is so enigmatic for the narrator, there is that so-called "white ink," that sustenance of her people. Can it be that Kafka's mouse is not only a female, but also a feminist?

Just as we readers know that Josefine is female, we know that the mouse-narrator is male. This is obvious. But what is it in the text that makes it so clear? How do we know that the narrator is male, once we dismiss the notion that the narrator is Kafka? Does he think and thus write like a man? The answer is purely and simply, yes! The male perspective of his narration is striking. First, from the start, his style is that of a possessive spokes*man* of his people: "Our singer is called Josephine." ". . . as we are not in general a music-loving race," ". . . our life is hard" (360). He is speaking from the standpoint of a center and this center is always man. It is Josefine who is set against the group, who is decentered, peripheral, a satellite, a moon. Each of her characteristics is set within a context of being different. Often in the course of narrating, he suggests he is part of a community: "Among intimates we admit freely to one another . . ." (360); "when she makes such an appearance, we who are supposed to be her opponents are in the habit of saying . . ." (364), etc. Even though this is a thinking mouse, an intellectual mouse, a writing mouse, he is still part of a body of mousepeople, part of the same, whereas Josefine, even when she agrees, is different: "we admire in her what we do not at all admire in ourselves; in this respect, I may say, she is of one mind with us" (362). Another aspect of the male perspective in the narration is the narrator's self-conscious inability to comprehend Josefine. She seems to remain an enigma to him, one which he can never solve. He wants to grasp her meaning and, in so doing, gain control of her. He follows all possible ways of understanding and describing her, but he cannot define her essence.

Throughout the tale, there is also an undercurrent of desire. Josefine fascinates the narrator. She is a creature of marvel, just as the girl on the tram is for the narrator in Kafka's short piece by that name. There, the narrator studies in great detail a girl he sees, taking in her clothing, her features, right down to "the whole ridge of the whorl of her right ear." Finally, he wonders ". . . How is it that she is not amazed at herself, that she keeps her lips closed and makes no such remark?" (389). The mouse-narrator finds Josefine just as fascinating. So obsessed with defining her, he is clearly smitten by her—must see her, finds her delicate, and thinks: "It must be admitted that Josephine's way of thinking, like her figure, is often very charming" (374). In short, his is an obsession of desire. And like all desire, his stems from triangulation. He wants her because the mousefolk want her. She is the object of all their desire, and in the narrator's attempt to capture her being in words, Josefine becomes, at the same time, a unified and self-contradictory concept. Because the mouse-narrator desires all things in her, she is finally obliterated from the text. . . .

In "Josefine" the narrator cannot speak of any subject without invoking at every turn the elements of a preexisting language referring to that subject—defining it and legitimizing any statements about it. To be sure, Josefine is an intersection of discourses, as we have said before, but the road most heavily travelled is the discourse on her gender, which, in fact, is hardly explicitly invoked at all. However, in virtually every statement, elements that unmistakeably pertain to the topoi of woman are mentioned. Normally, we would describe a certain woman in a certain way—good, evil, beautiful, ugly, charming, cruel—create an image of a simple or a complex individual, perhaps containing an occasional paradox and contradiction; this is all part of how the reality effect is manufactured. But in order to be realistic, that is to say plausible—*vraisemblable*—one must be selective—a certain woman must have certain characteristics. Therefore certain traits must be invoked and not others. In "Josefine," however, the narrator finds in his obsessive desire to capture and to express the nature of this creature, to represent, that is to say, her reality, her essence, finds himself swamped by the linguistic materials with which he must work to create her representation. The narrator, her alleged opponent, as we shall see, is increasingly captured not by Josefine's art, like the other folk, but rather by the materials of his own art. In saturating his discourse on Josefine with all of the elements of the discourse on woman, the subject at last disappears. The discourse has self-destructed, and Josefine loses and gains. What she loses is precisely what the discourse existed in order to grant her—her identity, her being apart. What she has gained is "[to] rise to the heights of redemption and be forgotten like all her brothers" (376).

Whatever is proverbially said about woman, the opposite is, for the most part, also said. Equivocating about woman is the nature of the discourse on woman. But one idea is unequivocal—woman is always different, both from man and from herself. To be more specific, the western discourse on women consists in effect in maintaining that women are both more and less, better and worse, higher and lower than men; women are the bridge-link between man and beast on the one hand, and man and angel on the other. At least since the Middle Ages, the double-edged topoi of woman as the daughter of Eve and the sister of Mary has formed a mode—one among an indefinitely large number of exempla—of this discourse.

When we examine the text of "Josefine" closely, we see many contradictory characteristics ascribed to Josefine. On the one hand, we are made to believe at the start that her singing is special: "There is no one but is carried away by her singing, . . ." (360), but in the next paragraph, we are told that "Josephine's singing, as singing, is nothing out of the ordinary" (361). The narrator remarks upon her delicacy, yet in the same paragraph, he describes her as being "actually vulgar" (362). Josefine wants things on her own terms, yet this includes all disturbances being very welcome to her—"Da kommen ihr denn alle Störungen sehr gelegen."[2] She is capable of a "piping sound that despite all rehearsal was still very tentative" (". . . das trotz aller Routine immer noch schüchterne Pfeifen. . ." [196]) yet in the same paragraph she strikes up "triumphal notes." When she sings, it appears ". . . as if while she is so wholly withdrawn and living only in her song a cold breath blowing upon her might kill her" (363), yet if she does not get things her own way, ". . . then indeed she turns furious, then she stamps her feet, swearing in most unmaidenly fashion; she actually bites" (364). The narrator continues in this manner. He compares Josefine to a child ". . . it is rather a thoroughly childish way of doing, and childish gratitude" (366). Yet, in times of trouble, the mice all come together, huddle close to each other around Josefine; ". . . it is as if we were drinking in all haste . . . from a cup of peace in common before the battle" (367). More like a mother than any child, Josefine sustains her people in perilous times. This dimension of her character is shown again when the narrator describes the mice at her concerts in times of stress: "Here in the brief intervals between their struggles our people dream, it is as if the limbs of each were loosened, as if the harried individual once in a while could relax and stretch himself at ease in the great, warm bed of the community" (370). Josefine's concerts are like a brief return to the womb for the mice people. She takes on the role of a kind of "primal mother" in whose music her people find something of their childhood: "Something of our poor brief childhood is in it, something of lost happiness that can never be found again . . ." (370).

As the mouse-narrator progresses in his tale, the pace of Josefine's double-edged attributes intensifies. At one point he tells us: ". . . she says very little . . . she is silent among the chatterers . . ." (366). But later when he relates that Josefine wants to be excused from daily chores, he remarks that till now she has waged her battles only with words: ". . . sie [hat] ihn [den Kampf] bisher nur durch Worte geführt . . ." (206). Although the title has told us the story is about Josefine, the singer, he later explains that the mouse-people listen to her precisely because she is "no singer." In the same paragraph he talks about Josefine's intuition about herself, but then in the same sentence, ". . . only she keeps on singing and piping her intuition away" (368). She is described as a pacifist opiate: he quotes her followers, ". . . how else could you explain the great audiences, especially when danger is most imminent, which have even often enough hindered proper precautions being taken in time to avert danger" (370). But in these times, Josefine becomes a coward, takes cover and disappears. The narrator comments that "[she] has always occupied the safest place and was always the first to whisk away quietly and speedily under cover of her escort" (371). But Josefine can do what she pleases. In other words, she is irresponsible, and yet "she will be forgiven for everything." The law is for others, not for Josefine. She is beyond it. Josefine, we are told, wants exemption from all daily work. Her argument is that "she has to exhaust her strength completely" in working and singing, yet to try and get out of work, ". . . for this purpose her strength seems inexhaustible . . ." (372). Immediately after telling us what Josefine has said, the narrator affirms that what Josefine really wants is not what she puts into words: "Nun ist es ja klar, dass Josefine nicht eigentlich das anstrebt, was sie wörtlich verlangt" (205). Her language must be interpreted by those who understand her better than she does herself. And this kind of "paternal care" is extended even to protecting her from herself. After all, she is clearly paranoid: "If she really had enemies . . . But she has no enemies . . ." (372).

The narrator's last few paragraphs pile attribute upon attribute. Trying to account for Josefine's behavior, the narrator inserts the idea of Josefine's age as a factor, which he himself immediately dismisses: "For her there is no growing old and no falling off in her voice" (373). She uses "the most unworthy methods." In other words, he finds her bold and sneaky, yet he says, "It must be admitted that Josephine's way of thinking, like her figure, is often very charming" (374). She changes her mind, for instance when she cuts out the grace notes, then reinserts them, then removes them again, yet, says the narrator, "Josephine, however, does not give in" (375). For all her changeability, she is steadfast. Finally, shortly before her disappearance, Josefine gets up to sing, feigns illness, is carried onto the stage by her followers— her *Anhang*—and bursts "inexplicably into tears," yet at the end of her performance, she measures her audience ". . . with cold eyes" (375). The narrator finds her "mistaken . . . in her calculations" and "clever," but raises the possibility that she may be driven on by destiny.

In his narration of Josephine, the mouse-narrator has created a character who is extraordinary and not extraordinary, delicate and vulgar, particular and easy-going, frail and strong, a child and a mother, quiet and loud, a singer and no singer, exhaustible and inexhaustible, aging and ageless, sneaky and charming, changeable and steadfast, emotional and calculating. A character who is both more and less than herself. A small, frail little mouse with a voice that makes her larger than life.

1. Franz Kafka, *Franz Kafka: The Complete Stories*, ed. Nahum N. Glatzer (New York: Schocken Books, Inc., 1971), 360. All subsequent quotations from this story are cited in English in the text, with the page number from this edition replacing the original German.

2. *Franz Kafka: Sämtliche Erzählungen*, ed. Paul Raabe (Frankfurt am Main, 1970), 196. All German quotations from the story are cited in the text with the page number from this edition.

"In the Penal Colony": Kafka's Unorthodox Theology

*Doreen F. Fowler**

An explorer visiting a penal colony is introduced to two orders—the old and the new. The old order instituted a harsh, merciless system of justice; the new order favors a milder doctrine. At the time of the present action of "In the Penal Colony" the new order is gradually replacing the old. The old Commandant, who founded and promulgated the old order, is dead, and the officer is the last ardent champion of the old tradition.

As the story opens, the explorer is about to witness an execution which typifies the old order's stern judicial procedure. The explorer becomes concerned when he learns that the condemned man has had no opportunity to defend himself and is in almost total ignorance of his crime and his sentence. Even more disturbing to the explorer is the nature of the condemned man's offense. He has failed to perform a meaningless and nearly impossible observance: "It is his duty, you see, to get up every time the hour strikes and salute the captain's door."[1] Finally, the explorer is told the officer's guiding principle in all matters related to justice: "Guilt is never to be doubted" (198).

Having explained the central tenet of the old order's judicial process, the officer describes how the piercing writing of a deadly machine inexorably metes out justice on the body of the condemned man:

> And then the execution began! No discordant noise spoilt the working of the machine. Many did not care to watch it but lay with closed eyes in the sand; they all knew: Now Justice is being done. . . . Well, and then came the sixth hour! It was impossible to grant all the requests to be allowed to watch it from near by. The Commandant in his wisdom ordained that the children should have the preference; I, of course, because of my office had the privilege of always being at hand; often enough I would be squatting there with a small child in either arm. How we all absorbed the look of transfiguration on the face of the sufferer, how we bathed our cheeks in the radiance of that justice, achieved at last and fading so quickly! What times these were, my comrade!" (209)

*This excerpt is reprinted by permission from *College Literature* 6, no. 2 (Spring 1979):113–120, and the author.

Even at this early stage in the unfolding narrative, it is possible to discern the essence of the old order: human existence is essentially characterized by guilt, and justice demands the terrible agony of the machine.

In the course of describing the old order's judicial procedure the officer beseeches the explorer to assist him in preserving the old tradition. The explorer, after a moment's hesitation, refuses this request. Faced with this rejection, the officer announces, "Then the time has come" (217); he frees the condemned man and takes his place on the torturing device. The execution then proceeds with this substitution of the officer for the condemned man. The officer is clearly a willing sacrifice to the apparatus: "Everything was ready, only the straps hung down at the sides, yet they were obviously unnecessary, the officer did not need to be fastened down" (227). The machine, however, fails to function properly, and the anticipated moment of transfiguring justice is not experienced: "And here, almost against his will, he had to look at the face of the corpse. It was as it had been in life; no sign was visible of the promised redemption; what the others had found in the machine the officer had not found" (224–25).

"In the Penal Colony" concludes with the explorer's departure from the colony. Before leaving, the explorer visits the grave of the old Commandant, which is located under a table in a teahouse. The explorer is told that the officer had attempted "several times to dig the old man up by night, but he was always chased away" (224). The inscription on the grave of the old Commandant reads: "Here rests the old Commandant. His adherents, who now must be nameless, have dug this grave and set up this stone. There is a prophecy that after a certain number of years the Commandant will rise again and lead his adherents from this house to recover the colony. Have faith and wait!" (226). Immediately after this visit to the old Commandant's grave, the explorer leaves the penal colony, driving away the soldier and the condemned man who seek to depart with him.

Implicit in this summary of the narrative developments of "In the Penal Colony" are a number of striking analogues to Biblical events and religious doctrines. The old order, which is the central subject of "In the Penal Colony," immediately evokes a comparison to the old tradition of the Old Testament—the "Old Law." . . .

Once an analogy between the old order and the Hebraic tradition is recognized, it is immediately clear that the old Commandant represents God-the-Father, the Creator of the Genesis account. Like the

God of Genesis, who created the earth, the old Commandant invented the torture machine and is responsible for the entire structure of the penal colony. In the words of the officer: "This apparatus was invented by our former Commandant. . . . Well, it isn't saying too much if I tell you that the organization of the whole penal colony is his work" (193). By means of this analogy between the old Commandant and the God of Genesis, Kafka clearly implies that our world is like a penal colony, and even more specifically (because the torture machine represents a microcosm of the penal colony), like the torture machine. This parallel suggests that the world, like the torture machine, was created to induce the suffering necessary for the expiation of human guilt.

The belief that guilt is inherent in existence and that men live to expiate this guilt by suffering is clearly evident in other works of Kafka—*The Trial* and "The Judgment." The appearance of identical ideas in these works substantiates the assertion that an analogy between the torture machine and the earth is suggested in "In the Penal Colony."

Just as the penal colony's old order evokes a Biblical parallel, so also does the new order. At first glance, the new regime might seem to resemble the Hellenistic tradition which Matthew Arnold describes as both opposing and alternating with the Hebraic tradition in the course of history. Like the Hellenistic tradition, the new order is mild, is opposed to torture as a means to human salvation, and does not stress human guilt and sinfulness. However, the terminology that Kafka employs to describe the new order clearly points to an analogy with the New Testament tradition or the "New Law." The new tradition is described as "our new, mild doctrine" (207), and it is the order approved of by "the ladies" (208), suggesting an association with love and gentleness. Clearly such descriptions are meant to evoke Christ's new law of love, which contrasts with the sterner law of the Old Testament. Finally, just as the new law of the Christian tradition follows the harsher, old law of the Hebraic tradition, so also in "In the Penal Colony" the new order follows a harsher former order.

Once this connection is understood, it becomes apparent that the Christ-figure in Kafka's Biblical analogy is the officer. Like God-the-Son who existed from time immemorial with God-the-Father and who aided in the creation of the world, the officer contributed to the institution of the penal colony from its inception: "I assisted at the very earliest experiments and had a share in all the work until its completion" (193). Like Christ, son of God-the-Father, the officer pays filial-like devotion and allegiance to the old Commandant. The officer's youth further reinforces this resemblance to God-the-Son. Finally, the officer's willing sacrifice of himself in the place of the condemned man clearly suggests an analogy to Christ's suffering and death, which, according to Christian theology, were accomplished in order to redeem condemned humanity from the effects of original sin.

With the suggestion of this last correspondence, Kafka's divergent interpretation of New Testament theology becomes fully apparent. The New Testament affirms that Christ died in order to free humanity from bondage to original sin. According to Kafka's construction of Biblical events, as suggested in "In the Penal Colony," Christ died for an opposite reason—in affirmation of man's guilt and the necessity of suffering for that guilt. The Christ-figure of Kafka's analogy, the officer, sacrifices himself in order to bear witness to the old order that identifies guilt with human existence and justice with punishment. *Thus, in Kafka's inversion of traditional Christian theology, Christ is not the originator of a new law of love and forgiveness. Rather, Kafka's Christ-figure is the last proponent of the old, stern law which decrees that atonement for human guilt is won only by suffering.* Implicit in "In the Penal Colony," then, is Kafka's own personal construction of Biblical events. Christian theology teaches that Christ willingly submitted to torture and crucifixion in order to expiate man's burden of sin and guilt. The Christ-figure of Kafka's analogy suffers and dies in order to affirm that only by such suffering and death is human sinfulness to be overcome.

Kafka's frequently reiterated feelings of guilt and inferiority may provide an explanation for this unique interpretation of Biblical events. It is widely acknowledged that Kafka was overawed by his father, and that he also magnified and deplored his own limitations. For example, in the "Letter to My Father" Kafka writes: "In front of you I lost my self-confidence and exchanged it for an infinite sense of guilt. In the recollection of this infinity I once wrote about someone, quite truly, 'He is afraid the shame will even live on after him.'"[2] To Kafka, who was overwhelmed by a sense of guilt, the Christian doctrine that Christ's crucifixion freed man from the effects of original sin might very possibly have seemed remote and unreal, and, because Kafka was filled with dread and fear of authority figures, the Christian vision of God as a loving redeemer might also have seemed untenable. Thus the meanings attached to Biblical events by Kafka's skillful manipulation of analogies in "In the Penal Colony" might represent an interpretation of Sacred Scripture uniquely suited to a man of Franz Kafka's temperament.

One final Biblical parallel in "In the Penal Colony" remains to be interpreted—the inscription on the grave of the old Commandant which prophesies his resurrection, return, and resumption of power. This prophecy clearly recalls the resurrection of the New Testament and the Biblical prophecy of Christ's second coming. Here, as elsewhere, however, these Biblical parallels are infused with unorthodox meanings. The New Testament describes the resurrection as Christ's triumphant victory over sin and death (St. Paul writes to the Corinthians: "If Christ had not risen then vain is our teaching and vain is your faith"[3]) and the second coming as the return of a loving redeemer. In "In the Penal Colony" the resurrection and the second coming both refer to the return of the old order espoused by both Kafka's God-the-Father-figure, the old Commandant, and Kafka's Christ-figure, the officer. Thus, the inscription's words, "the Commandant will rise again and lead his adherents from this house to recover the colony," clearly indicate that the resurrection and second coming in "In the Penal Colony" will herald the return of the old, stern system of lifelong punishment for intrinsic human sinfulness. By this manipulation of Biblical analogues, Kafka suggests his own personal interpretation of Biblical events. For Kafka, the second coming will not bring the return of a resurrected, loving redeemer, but the return of a harsh and unforgiving system of justice.

1. Franz Kafka, *The Penal Colony; Stories and Short Pieces* (New York: Shocken Books, 1948), 198. All subsequent references to "In the Penal Colony" are to this edition.

2. "Letter to My Father," in *Franz Kafka: An Autobiography*, by Max Brod (New York: Schocken Books, 1937), 24.

3. St. Paul, First Letter to the Corinthians, 1:15.

William J. Dodd

Kafka and Freud: A Note on *In der Strafkolonie*

*William J. Dodd**

The execution apparatus in *In der Strafkolonie* ["In the Penal Colony"] is perhaps the most memorable of Kafka's many vivid inventions. The aim of this note is to suggest a possible level of association implicit in Kafka's description of the machine, and so to throw some light on the meaning of the story. As the officer enthusiastically explains the machine's parts to the somewhat inattentive traveler, the rhythm of Kafka's text seems to hint that something significant is being discussed: "It consists, as you see, of three parts. In the course of time each of these parts has acquired a kind of popular nickname. The lower one is called the 'Bed,' the upper one the 'Designer,' and this one here in the middle that moves up and down is called the 'Harrow' [*Egge*]."[1] We follow the straying thoughts of the traveler's distracted mind for several moments before the officer replies: "Yes, the Harrow . . . a good name for it." At this point Kafka's "careful technique of suggestive hints" begins.[2] The officer explains that the name derives from the arrangement of the needles and the part's general resemblance to a harrow. But let us weigh the thrice-repeated word *Egge*. The part of the machine so named is, in the officer's words, "der mittlere, schwebende Teil"—the middle, hovering part, or perhaps we should say *wavering* part. That this middle part of the machine "hovers/wavers" above the bed and below the designer prompts the speculation that Kafka may be making an ironic allusion to the divisions of consciousness postulated by psychoanalysis, and particularly to Freud's hypotheses which he eventually developed into a scheme comprising *das Ich, das Es*, and *das Überich* [the ego, the id, and the superego].

Indeed the overall mechanism of the apparatus in this story seems succinctly and consistently to incorporate an ironic allusion to Freud's scheme of consciousness. *Die Egge*, situated in the middle of the apparatus, not only shares this location with the *Ich* [ego] in Freud's scheme; it is also linked to it by a phonetic association exactly like those explored by Freud: thus *Ich—ego—Egge*. Not only does the *Egge*

*Excerpted from *Monatshefte* 70, no. 2 (Summer 1978):129–37. Reprinted by permission of the University of Wisconsin Press.

vacillate (a token, perhaps, of the ego's inherent insubstantiality and insecurity), but it does so in a state of inertia, determined by the opposing thrusts of the *Bett* [bed] beneath it (the luxuriant habitat of the unconscious life, of animal pleasures and physical warmth) and the *Zeichner* [designer] above it, that part of the apparatus which determines the patterning of the message to be imprinted via the *Egge* on the flesh of the victim. The designer's location and its function as the source of *Gewissensbisse* [remorse] complete the scheme of allusion to the Freudian psyche. The interiority of this scheme of allusion is implied in the officer's first words—the story's opening words—"It's a remarkable [*eigentümlicher*] piece of apparatus," in which the inherent double meaning of "eigentümlich" (both *merkwürdig* [remarkable] and *innewohnend* [inherent to]) is exploited in a way which is typical of Kafka's ironic technique.

In order to explore the suggestion that in the execution apparatus Kafka is in part alluding to the structure of the Freudian consciousness, let us take as our model *The Interpretation of Dreams*, first published in 1900, and by 1914 in its fourth edition. It is likely that Kafka knew this work, and it will be seen that it contains much potential grist to Kafka's mill, in as much as it furnishes some fine examples of how suggestive Freud's terms, how pregnant his procedure could have been for a mind like Kafka's. It also provides some interesting, more specific points of comparison.

In the seventh chapter of *The Interpretation of Dreams*, "The Psychology of the Dream Processes," Freud had set as his task "to set up a number of fresh hypotheses which touch tentatively upon the structure of the apparatus of the mind [*seelischen Apparats*] and upon the play of forces operating in it. We must be careful, however, not to pursue these hypotheses too far beyond their logical links, or their value will be lost in uncertainties."[3] Of immediate interest here is Freud's reference to the apparatus of consciousness, "der seelische Apparat," which during the course of the chapter is variously referred to as "das Seeleninstrument," "der psychische Apparat," "das seelische Instrument," and "dieses allerwunderbarste und allergeheimnisvollste Instrument" [this most wonderful and all mysterious Instrument], and Freud's attempt to picture "the play of forces operating in it." Freud goes on to emphasize that these terms should be accepted only in so far as they help elucidate the structure and processes of consciousness in this as yet uncharted area of investigation:

> Analogies of this kind are only intended to assist us in our attempt to make the complications of mental functioning intelligible by dissecting the function and assigning its different constituents to different component parts of the apparatus. So far as I know, the experiment has not hitherto been made of using this method of dissection in order to investigate the way in which the mental instrument is put together, and I can see no harm in it. We are justified, in my view, in giving free rein to our speculations so long as we retain the coolness of our judgment and do not mistake the scaffolding for the building. And since at our first approach to something unknown all that we need is the assistance of provisional ideas, I shall give preference in the first instance to hypotheses of the crudest and most concrete description. (536)

This is an admonition, however, which for some readers may tend to be superseded by the persistently visual quality of Freud's presentation. With hindsight it seems likely that Freud's use of spatial metaphor and mechanical analogy to lend visual immediacy to "the construction and working methods of the mental instrument" (511) would suggest itself strongly to Kafka's richly associative and vividly pictorial imagination, the *modus operandi* of which was precisely "[to] mistake the scaffolding for the building" (536).

Moreover, Freud's attitude to the "Unbekanntes" [the unknown] with which he is dealing, his self-assured manner, his attempt to explain the functioning of the mental apparatus from an analysis of its component parts—"intended to assist us in our attempt to make the complications of mental functioning intelligible by dissecting the function and assigning its different constituents to different component parts of the apparatus" (536) (which could also refer to the way in which the officer sets about explaining his apparatus to the uninitiated traveler in Kafka's story)—indeed, Freud's whole approach to his research could have found a response to Kafka, who, however, as *In der Strafkolonie* demonstrates, could not agree that the issues involved were "*harmlos*" [no harm].

Freud's tactic of treating the psyche as if it were a topographical structure with spatial properties and component parts arranged in a particular interrelationship leads him to compare the structure of this apparatus to that of a compound instrument ("zusammengesetztes Instrument") such as a camera or a microscope, and to a reflex apparatus ("Reflexapparat"): "Accordingly, we will picture the mental apparatus as a compound instrument, to the components of which we will give the name of 'agencies' [*Instanzen*], or (for the sake of greater clarity) 'systems'" (536–37). It is interesting to note here the officer's apologetic explanation to the traveler in Kafka's story when the hand-strap on the apparatus tears: "This is a very complex [*zusammengesetzt*] machine, it can't be helped that things are breaking or giving way here and there . . ." (151). Kafka's apparatus is also "zusammengesetzt," and in a sense—in the way it accommodates itself to the condemned man's physical dimensions, posture and movements—it is a "Reflex-apparat," too. The fact that Freud uses the term *Instanzen*, with its legal overtones, for the agencies of consciousness (he postulates "a principle of appellate procedure [*ein Prinzip des Instanzenzugs*] that seems to govern the structure of the apparatus"[4]) would certainly have been pregnant with meaning for Kafka; and here we have the possibility that Freud's scheme of the mind could have fused suggestively with Kafka's awareness of the legal metaphor as a vehicle for his preoccupation with the theme of guilt and judgment.

At the beginning of chapter 7(f) "The Unconscious and Consciousness-Reality," Freud calls the reader's attention once more to the inadequacy of the spatial metaphor, with its implication of psychic localities, and seeks to replace it with the idea of cathexis ("Energiebesetzung"). This, Freud explains, avoids misconceptions about the "location" of the two unconscious systems (at this stage in Freud's theory, the Unconscious and the Preconscious) which may arise "so long as we looked upon the two systems in the most literal and crudest sense as two localities in the mental apparatus" (610). He warns against "every idea of a change of locality," and suggests:

> Let us replace these metaphors by something that seems to correspond better to the real state of affairs, and let us say instead that some particular mental grouping has had a cathexis of energy attached to it or withdrawn from it, so that the structure in question has come under the sway of a particular agency or been withdrawn from it. What we are doing here is once again to replace a topographical way of representing things by a dynamic one. What we regard as mobile is not the psychical structure itself but its innervation. (610–11)

Freud's replacing of the topographical scheme with a dynamic one also introduces material which could have attracted Kafka. The fact that the *Zeichner* [designer] and the *Bett* [bed] in Kafka's apparatus are powered by electrical batteries, for instance, takes on an ironic significance if regarded in this connection. "Now listen,"says the officer to the traveler, "Both the Bed and the Designer have an electric battery each; the Bed needs one for itself, the Designer for the Harrow" (143). This remark is one of those strange, isolated details in Kafka's writing which strike the reader as odd, in that they seem appended to rather than integral to the story. The suggestion that Kafka had in mind a system of allusion to the workings of the Freudian psyche may indeed explain the puzzling intrusion of this remark.

These examples taken from *The Interpretation of Dreams* show how readily Freud's metaphors and images—introduced somewhat defensively, in the cause of science—can be set alongside Kafka's fantastic invention, once we accept the principle of the ironic allusion in Kafka. That *The Interpretation of Dreams* should be considered a "source" must remain an interesting speculation; but it seems certain that, in the execution apparatus, Kafka is incorporating subtly concealed allusions to Freud's "psychic apparatus."

Clearly, the officer does not intend his apparatus to be understood in terms of Freud's "psychic apparatus." It seems certain that he speaks in complete ignorance of the interpretation which could be placed on his description by a European traveler (or reader!), and it is here that Kafka's subtle irony is at its most profound. The three-fold scheme is, after all, a recurrent feature of man's myths, ancient and modern; and underlying the tension between the old and modern interpretations of existence which is at the center of *In der Strafkolonie* there is an implicit parallel drawn between their tripartite structures. The three parts of the mechanism as understood by the Old Commandant were not, or not exclusively, encompassed by the concept of consciousness, but belonged to an older mode of interpreting life which acknowledged the existence of a suprahuman *Instanz*. This system has now fallen into decay, as if in confirmation of Zarathustra's pronouncement (it is interesting to note in this respect that, in Freud's use of the words, "seelisch" and "psychisch" are synonymous), and is now a forgotten and discarded, though not yet "toothless" credo which has to do not with the agencies of consciousness but with the reality of the I of the individual human soul poised between Good and Evil, God and the Devil. It was in an age when this conception of life was regarded as self-evident that the Old Commandant designed and constructed his contraption for use in a world which was, quite incontestably, a penal institution.

The fact, mentioned fleetingly during the traveler's lapse in concentration in the third paragraph of the story and so easily overlooked as a strangely insignificant detail, that "the officer was speaking French," (142) may point to yet another well-concealed verbal association. For in the word *Bett* [bed], given throughout—as are all the officer's words—in German, there is a phonetic association with the Grand Designer's beast opponent, *la bête noire*. It may be objected that this is an arcane connection, for the officer at no time says the phoneme *Bett-bête*, but presumably uses the French *lit*. Since the story is mediated throughout in German the association is certainly circuitous, a concatenated, trans-lingual pun (thus *lit-Bett-bête*); but this kind of association, it should be repeated, is both typical of Kafka's technique and perfectly "Freudian."

The associations which radiate from the component parts of the execution apparatus are thus both subtly concealed and central to the story as a whole. The three-tier system brings together and contrasts two systems by means of which man has tried to come to terms with his existence. The *Zeichner* [designer] symbolically represents the Grand Designer of the universe, but also corresponds to the psychic agency of conscience. At the opposite, lower end of the construction, the *Bett* [bed] suggests *la bête noire*, the Devil; and also the region of primal instincts which Freud was to call the "Id." In the middle of these conflicting forces, the *Egge* [harrow] corresponds to the individual soul in the first system, and to the "ego" in the second. This may be an esoteric interpretation, but we would suggest that, at a deep level, much of the story's meaning and value inheres in the subtly engineered juxtaposition of esoteric and exoteric interpretations of the apparatus itself, and that this is a prime source of irony in the story.

The suggestion that details of the execution apparatus incorporate ironic allusions to the "psychic apparatus" enhances the comic and grotesque possibilities of the story. The officer's habit of clambering about the apparatus making minor adjustments and repairs with a screwdriver, for example, and his casual remark "Things sometimes go wrong, of course" (141), perhaps even his addressing the traveler as "a famous Western investigator" (156) acquire a quite specific ironic force. The officer's remark to the traveler: "You will have seen similar apparatus in hospitals [*Heilanstalten*], but in our Bed the movements are

Walter H. Sokel

all precisely calculated; you see, they have to correspond very exactly to the movements of the Harrow" (143–44), points fairly overtly to a comparison between theology and psychoanalysis in its therapeutic phase by exploiting the associated meanings of *Heil* [well, cured]. The allusion to the Freudian subconscious and its essential indeterminacy is indeed particularly clear here, as is the comparison (but note "*ähnlich*") of psychological and theological machinery. Once one accepts the network of allusion, the text begins to radiate moments of revelation. . . .

1. *Franz Kafka: The Complete Stories*, ed. Nahum N. Glatzer (New York: Schocken Books, 1971), 141–42. All subsequent quotations from this story are cited in English in the text, with the page number from this edition replacing the original German.

2. Franz Kafka, *Der Heizer . . .* , ed. M. Pasley (Cambridge, 1966), 21.

3. Sigmund Freud, *The Interpretation of Dreams*, ed. and trans. James Strachey (New York: Basic Books, 1955), 511. All subsequent quotations from this work are cited in English in the text, with the page number from this edition replacing the original German.

4. *Die Traumdeutung*, fourth enlarged edition, with contributions by Otto Rank (Leipzig/Vienna: Deuticke, 1914), 477. Editor's translation.

From Marx to Myth: The Structure and Function of Self-Alienation in Kafka's "Metamorphosis"
*Walter H. Sokel**

Kafka's uniqueness as a narrative author lies, among other things, in the literalness with which the metaphors buried in linguistic usage come alive and are enacted in the scenes he presents. The punishing machine devised by the Old Commander in *The Penal Colony*, for instance, engraves the law that the condemned have transgressed on their minds by imprinting it literally on their flesh. By the appellation

*This excerpt is reprinted by permission of the author from *The Literary Review*, 26, no. 4 (Summer 1983):485–95.

"vermin," linguistic usage designates the lowest form of human self-contempt. Seeing himself as vermin, and being treated as such by his business and family, the travelling salesman Gregor Samsa literally turns into vermin.

Kafka's narratives enact not only the metaphors hidden in ordinary speech, but also ideas crucial in the history of thought. "The Metamorphosis" is a striking example. Gregor Samsa's transformation into vermin presents self-alienation in a literal way, not merely a customary metaphor become fictional fact. The travelling salesman wakes up one morning and cannot recognize himself. Seeing himself as a gigantic specimen of vermin, he finds himself in a fundamental sense estranged from himself. No manner more drastic could illustrate the alienation of a consciousness from its own being than Gregor Samsa's startled and startling awakening.

The idea of human self-alienation has played a crucial role in modern thought from German classical Idealism to Marxism and Existentialism. First encountered in the thought of Wilhelm von Humboldt, Schiller, Fichte, and Hegel, and subsequently in Feuerbach and Marx, this idea always implies the individual's estrangement (*Entfremdung*) from his humanity or "human species being," i.e., from the individual's membership in the human species. The individual is estranged from himself insofar as he is alienated from his essential nature as a human being.

Rooted as he was in German Idealism and the tradition of German classical literature, the young Marx saw the essential nature of the human species residing in freely productive activity. Human species-being was for him the production of objects that were literally *Gegenstände*, things that having issued from the labor of his hands and mind now face their producer as the objects of his world. Thus the human species is defined by world-creating or world-modifying activity. It is an activity that by virtue of its productive inventiveness humanizes nature. In order to be truly human, this praxis must be, at least partly, self-determined. Work must be engaged in for its own sake. It must have been chosen, partially at least, for its intrinsic pleasure. It must not merely be dictated by external need or the commands of others. In exact analogy to Immanuel Kant's corollary to the categorical imperative, which defines genuine morality, genuinely human labor for Marx must be at least partially its own end, its own freely chosen purpose, and not entirely "a means" for something else such as the satisfaction of extrinsic needs or the insurance of mere survival. To qualify as truly human, labor must always have an element of free choice. It must, at least partly, be its own reward and satisfaction. "At any time" it must "be considered its own purpose, an end in itself."

This freedom of doing one's work for its own sake, for the joy it affords the worker, is the factor that, according to Marx, distinguishes human from animal productivity. Animals, Marx observes, "produce only under the compulsion of physical need. Man, on the other hand, produces even when he is free of physical need, and only in this freedom is he humanly creative. . . . Such production is his active species being. By virtue of it, nature itself appears as man's creation and his reality."[1] Only where work appears as its own reward are human beings truly human. Where it is imposed solely by economic necessity, the worker is not merely alienated from himself as an individual; he is estranged from his humanity. Marx's idea of human self-alienation is not restricted to factory work, but includes any kind of work in which an individual is engaged merely for the wage or income it brings him. The worker is dehumanized wherever his work fails to involve his creative urge and desire.

Here we have arrived at the pre-history of Gregor Samsa's metamorphosis, as the reader learns from Gregor's reminiscences of and meditations about his job as a travelling salesman. We learn that Gregor had been estranged from himself in his all-consuming work even before he finds himself literally estranged from his bodily being. Gregor had found his work unbearable. He had longed for nothing more passionately than to leave his job, after telling the head of his firm his true opinion of this job. Gregor's profound self-alienation corresponds, with uncanny precision, to Marx's definition of the "externalization" of work under capitalism: "his work is *external* to the worker, i.e., it does not form part of his essential being so that instead of feeling well in his work, he feels unhappy, instead of developing his free physical and mental energy, he abuses his body and ruins his mind" (I, 564).

Gregor Samsa's professional activity has obviously been such purely instrumental work, external to himself, imposed upon him by the necessity of bailing out his bankrupt family, supporting them, and paying back his parents' debt to the boss of his firm. It is not only joyless and uncreative, it is totally determined by needs external to itself and Gregor. Freedom of creativeness—according to Marx the essence of truly human labor—finds an outlet in Samsa's life, prior to his metamorphosis, only in the carpentry in which he indulges in free evenings. Parenthetically we might recall that Kafka himself hated his bureaucrat's desk job because it served as a mere means to a purpose totally extrinsic to itself, namely a relatively short work day, and found by contrast genuine satisfaction in carpentering and gardening, activities chosen for their own sake, which, like writing, united creativeness with the satisfaction of inner needs.

Compared to accusations of his office work found in his autobiographical documents, Kafka's story, "The Metamorphosis," "systematizes," as it were, the Marxist factor, not by conscious design, of course, but by virtue of the astonishing parallelism in the point of view, particularly the presentation of self-alienation. Gregor's sole reason for enduring the hated position, the need to pay his parents' "debt" to his boss, drastically highlights the doubly extrinsic purpose of Gregor's work. For not only is his labor alien to his true desires, but its sole purpose, its fruit—the salary or commission that it affords him—does not even belong to him. Gregor's toil does not serve his own existence. It is not his own *Lebensmittel,* to use Marx's term—if left to himself, he would have quit long before—it belongs to and serves another.

This other is Gregor's father. He is the non-working beneficiary and exploiter of Gregor's labor. The product of this labor is the money which Gregor brings home. This money belongs to the other who does not work himself, but enjoys and disposes of the fruits of Gregor's work: "the money which Gregor had brought home every month—he himself had kept only a few pennies to himself—had not been used up completely and had accrued to form a small *capital*" (E, 97. Italics mine).[2] Gregor's father had expropriated the "surplus value" of Gregor's labor and formed with it his—to be sure, very modest—"capital." Gregor's relationship to his father thus represents an exact paradigm of the worker's exploitation by his capitalist employer, as described by Marx. The worker is alienated from the product of his labor because he has to yield it to the capitalist. The latter retains the lion's share for himself and returns to the worker only what the latter barely needs to survive. Through this despoiling of the fruits of his work the worker's existence becomes, in the words of Marx, "self-sacrifice and castigation" (I, 546): "In the last analysis, the extrinsic nature of his work is shown to the worker by the fact that his work is not his, but belongs to another. . . . it is the loss of his self" (I, 564f.). Gregor's metamorphosis literally enacts this "loss of self." It makes drastically visible the self-estrangement that existed even before his metamorphosis.

It is the father's "capital" that leaves Gregor tied to his servitude and bondage, for as the narrator says, "with this *surplus money* [Gregor] could have paid back a much larger part of his father's debt to his boss and the day on which he could have freed himself from his job would have been much closer. . ." (E, 97. Italics mine).

The last-mentioned fact represents a point at which an entirely different interpretative dimension intersects the Marxist framework of self-alienation that we have so far considered by itself. Although we have by no means as yet exhausted the parallelism between the Marxist concept of self-alienation and the structure and function of Gregor Samsa's metamorphosis in Kafka's text, we might state at this point that Kafka's "The Metamorphosis" is by no means completely defined, if merely seen as the literal enactment of self-alienation. Even if we were to restrict ourselves to this aspect, the centrality of the concept of self-alienation in modern thought would demand additional interpretative frameworks from which to approach Kafka's text, such as psychoanalytic, existentialist, biographical, linguistic, and phenomenological systems of reference which all must needs play important parts in a relatively comprehensive interpretation of Kafka's richly referential narrative.

However, what we shall consider now is Kafka's "The Metamorphosis" as the telling of a myth, for the mythic dimension relates to the Marxist one the way a picture frame relates to the picture which it contains and transcends, at one and the same time. In order to recognize this relationship, we shall have to consider the *mythos* of "The Metamorphosis." I use the term "mythos" in the Aristotelian sense as the whole chain of fictive events in their chronological as distinct from their narrated order.

The initial point of the mythos is not Gregor's transformation, but the business failure of Gregor's father five years before. This failure led to the contracting of the burdensome debt to the head of Gregor's firm. Thus the mythos begins with a family's cataclysmic fall into adversity through the fault of the father, more precisely the parents, since the text speaks of "die Schuld der Eltern" and only afterward of "die Schuld des Vaters." The German word *Schuld* signifies debt, guilt, and causative fault. This triple meaning is crucial to the understanding of Kafka's mythos. If understood in the sense of debt, the *Schuld* of Gregor's parents belongs to socio-economic quotidian reality. If understood in the two other senses, *Schuld* belongs to a framework of moral and religious values. The text's repeated use of the singular *Schuld* in contrast to the more customary plural *Schulden* for debt provides a sub-liminally effective counterpoint to the obvious surface meaning of the word.

This subliminal allusion to guilt receives corroboration from the position of "die Schuld der Eltern" ("the guilt of the parents") at the initial point of the narrative mythos. This position creates a subtle analogy to the fall of mankind as told in Genesis. To be sure, this analogy amounts to the faintest of hints. However, we cannot and must not avoid noting the allusion if we take seriously Kafka's view of language as expressed in one of his aphorisms: "Language can only be used allusively for anything outside the sensory world. . . ."[3]

The son of these guilty parents—Gregor—has to assume their guilt and pay it off "by the sweat of his countenance" (to quote Genesis), by his self-consuming drudgery for his parents' creditor. In the allusive context established by the semantic ambiguity of *Schuld*, Gregor's profoundly alienated existence prior to his metamorphosis establishes the parallel to man's fate after the expulsion from paradise. Like the children of Adam and Eve, Gregor through his sonship in the flesh has been condemned to a perennial debtor's existence. The two semantic realms of *Schuld*—debt and guilt—converge in the fateful consequence of the father's debt. With it, the father surrendered his family to a world in which the exploitation of man by man holds infernal sway. The world to which the father's failing has handed over his family is ruled by the principles of capitalist economics. In this world, the family ceases to be a family in the original and ideal sense of a community in which the bonds of blood—the *Blutkreis* to which Kafka in discussing "The Judgment" accords his highest respect—and natural affection prevail. Instead the family falls victim to the egotistical principle of *gegenseitige Übervorteilung* (mutual defrauding) in which Marx saw the governing principle of human life under capitalism.

Precisely because of his self-sacrifice in assuming his father's debt, Gregor rises to power as the breadwinner in his family and threatens to displace his father as the head of the household. This process reverses itself with Gregor's metamorphosis. Gregor's self-inflicted debasement entails his father's rejuvenation and return to power. These successive displacements—first the father's, then the son's—which find their parallel in Grete's ambiguous liberation through her brother's fall, have their contrastive complements in the parasitic exploitation of the winners by the losers. Before Gregor's metamorphosis, the father was the parasite. After the metamorphosis, the son assumes this role.

A world is shown in which the enjoyment of advantages by the one has to be purchased at the cost of the other. This is the world in a fallen state. Gregor's initial self-sacrifice through work whips up his pride in his ability to support his family in style. Those had been "happy times" when he had been able to "amaze and delight" his family by putting his hard-earned money on their table. But his self-surrender to his work causes a twofold alienation. Inwardly he remains estranged from his work because it is the kind of labor that cannot satisfy a human being. Outwardly his rise to power in the family overshadows the other members and results in their alienation from him. "A special warmth toward him was no longer forthcoming" (E, 98), so the text informs us. Long before his metamorphosis, Gregor and his family have lived coldly and incommunicatively side by side.

The metamorphosis reveals this alienation in its essence as *den völligen Verlust des Menschen* ("the total dehumanization of man") in which Marx saw the ultimate fate of man under capitalism. But it has another and ultimately more important function. Through it Gregor ceases to treat the *Schuld* of his parents as a debt that can be paid back by work, and assumes the *Schuld* in its deeper meaning. He no longer tries to pay back the *Schuld*; he incorporates it. With his incarnation he raises the narrative mythos from its socio-economic to its mythic meaning.

That Gregor's metamorphosis literally incarnates guilt becomes apparent first of all by the fact that his immediate reaction to his transformation is a guilty conscience. He has missed the hour of his work and feels guilty for it. He feels guilty for having plunged his family into misfortune. He is ashamed. He seeks to hide, to make himself invisible. But even apart from all subjectively felt or morally accountable guilt, guilt becomes evident in him objectively. For his transformation into vermin entails the crassest form of parasitic exploitation, a perfect turning of the tables on his family. His metamorphosis compels them to work for him and in his place. Because of him they will henceforth be "overlooked and overtired" (E, 112), condemned to suffer the fate of "paupers." To be sure, his father's bankruptcy five years before had condemned Gregor to an exploited existence. But by his metamorphosis, Gregor himself turns into an arch exploiter, the archetypal parasite which vermin represents. His very appearance as *ungeheueres Ungeziefer* is emblematic and flaunts a gigantic form of parasitism. Even as Gregor's subsequent daydream of declaring his love to his sister constitutes a gruesome parody of bourgeois-sentimental courtship, so his vermin existence as such embodies exploitation as the essence of human relations. By embodying parasitism in his shape, Gregor objectifies the guilt of his entire society. This guilt had originally shown itself in his father when he secretly cheated his son and furtively put aside his son's earnings to form "a modest capital." Reversing their roles, the son now becomes exploitation in its most honest, clearly visible form. To use T. S. Eliot's term, most appropriate to Kafka's tale, Gregor becomes the "objective correlative" of the insight that exploitation is the original guilt of mankind. Gregor literally becomes what his father had committed in stealthily performed acts. . . .

"The guilt of the parents" showed itself as indebtedness. It constituted capitulation to the world in its capitalist makeup. In strict consequence, economic determination inserts itself now into the myth as Kafka presents it. This insertion can be understood in socio-cultural and, indeed, Marxist categories. The plot inserted into the mythic events depicts a classic case of the proletarianization of a petty-bourgeois household. The "modest capital" created by the father's exploitation of Gregor's work for the firm "sufficed . . . . not at all to permit the family to live on its interests" (E, 97). In consequence the family loses its bourgeois status, its economic independence. Father Samsa remains the omnipotent potentate in his family. But in the world outside, he toils as a humble bank messenger. By the self-elimination of her brother as a human being, Grete rises to monopolistic eminence and privilege in her family. But in the outside world, she has to serve strangers as a poor sales girl. Gregor's mother is reduced to taking sewing and dress-making work home. In regard to the socio-economic world of exploited labor, Gregor, by the horrible paradox that is his metamorphosis, is now the only "free" member of the family, the only one who does not have to labor and let himself be exploited by the world outside. . . .

Since his metamorphosis, however, Gregor must assume the blame for this state of affairs. He alone now appears to be the cause of the whole "misfortune" of his family—unique as it is "in the entire circle of their relatives and acquaintances" (E, 112). He is guilty in a manner which lifts his "guilt" completely out of the sphere in which a socio-economic interpretation could still be relevant. To be sure, in consequence of its economic impoverishment, the family disintegrates as a natural community. So far the analogy to Marx's world view holds. However, the limits of such an analogy are reached as soon as we realize that the ultimate cause of this proletarianization is a circumstance

Walter H. Sokel

that transcends the observable laws of nature. In the midst of an environment which otherwise seems to be wholly determined by socioeconomic factors, Gregor's metamorphosis supplies the evidence of something inexplicable in, and therefore transcendent of, the terms of that *Weltbild*.

Mythic thinking also underlies Marx's view of history. Behind Marx's economic determinism one can glimpse the messianic martyr-savior's part played by the proletariat. In the world view of the young Marx especially, the proletariat suffers the fate and assumes the task of Christ. Today the proletariat is the scapegoat of humanity; tomorrow it will be its redeemer. So runs the Marxist myth. The proletariat will save the very society that has victimized it and committed the worst injustice against it. In his Preface to his "Critique of Hegel's *Philosophy of Law*," Marx states: "In order that *one single estate* may stand for the condition of the whole society, all the defects of that society must be concentrated in one . . . class; a particular estate must be the estate of general offense, must be the embodiment of all frustrations; one particular social class must be seen as the *notorious crime* of the whole society, so that liberation of this class will appear to be the universal self-liberation" (*I*, 501). In the microscopic society of his petty-bourgeois household, Gregor Samsa plays the same role that the proletariat, in Marx's vision, performs in the macroscopic social and universal society of the bourgeois-capitalist system. . . .

However, in sharp contrast to Marx, the optimistic "synthesis" of self-liberation and liberation of all others is totally lacking in Kafka's world. Marx's proletariat redeems itself by redeeming mankind. In Kafka, liberation can be achieved only by the total sacrifice, the self-eradication of the scapegoat. Only by vanishing completely can Gregor save his family and himself.

1. Karl Marx, *Frühe Schriften*, Erster Band, ed. Hans-Joachim Lieber and Peter Furth (Stuttgart: Cotta Verlag, 1962 [Karl Marx Ausgabe. Werke Schriften Briefe. Bd. I]), 567. My translation. Subsequent quotations are from this edition and translated by me. Volume and page numbers are cited in parentheses in the text immediately following the quotation.
2. *Erzählungen und kleine Prosa*, Gesammelte Schriften, Bd. I, ed. Max Brod, 2d. ed. (New York, Schocken Books, 1946 [1935]), 97. My translation. Subsequent quotations from Kafka's *The Metamorphosis* are from this edition

and translated by me. The page number is indicated in brackets in the text immediately following the quotation.

3. *Hochzeitsvorbereitungen auf dem Lande und andere Prosa aus dem Nachlass*, Gesammelte Werke, ed. Max Brod (New York: Schocken Books, 1953), 45. My translation.

Chronology

1883   Franz Kafka born 3 July in Prague, the first child of a German-Jewish family.

1901   Receives secondary school diploma (*Arbitur*) from the German Gymnasium of Prague.

1901–1906   University studies, first in German literature and then in law, culminating in a doctorate in jurisprudence from the German University.

1904   First version of "Description of a Struggle."

1907   Begins "Wedding Preparations in the Country."

1908   Publishes in the literary review *Hyperion* eight of the texts that would later appear in his first book, *Meditation*. Takes position with an insurance company that he will hold the rest of his life. Deepening friendship with Max Brod.

1909   The Prague newspaper *Bohemia* publishes "The Aeroplanes at Brescia."

1910   *Bohemia* prints five pieces later published in *Meditation*.

1911   Collaborates with Max Brod on *Richard and Samuel*.

1911–1912   First version of the novel *Verschollenen*, later called *Amerika* by Max Brod.

1912   Meets Felice Bauer in August, which will result in two engagements and more than seven hundred printed pages of letters to her over the next five years. Night of 22 September: the breakthrough during which he writes "The Judgment." Continues working on *Amerika* and writes "The Metamorphosis."

1912–1913   Works on "The Stoker" (first chapter of *Amerika*).

1913   Publication of *Meditation*, "The Judgment," and "The Stoker."

1914   Begins work on the unfinished novel, *The Trial*. Writes final, disconnected chapter of *Amerika*, "The Nature

Theater of Oklahoma," and "In the Penal Colony." Breaks engagement to Felice Bauer.

1915   Works on and abandons "The Village Schoolmaster"; works on "Blumfeld, an Elderly Bachelor." Publishes "The Metamorphosis."

1916–1917   Writes stories that will appear in *A Country Doctor* as well as a number of other texts that will be published posthumously.

1917   Is engaged to Felice for the second time but, upon discovering he has tuberculosis, breaks off the engagement in December. Writes "The Great Wall of China."

1918   Very ill with tuberculosis, also from the epidemic of Spanish influenza.

1919   Publishes "In the Penal Colony" and *A Country Doctor.* Writes, but does not deliver, the "Letter to His Father." Wants to marry Julie Wohryzek in spite of family opposition. Receives first letter from Milena Jesenská, who becomes his Czech translator.

1920   Love affair with Milena, friendship with the young poet Gustav Janouch (who will later publish transcriptions of their conversations). After three years of no writing, experiences a burst of creative energy and writes a good many short texts.

1921   After attempts at cure, takes permanent leave from his position.

1922   Begins and then abandons after several months the novel *The Castle.* Publishes "A Hunger Artist." Works on "The Investigations of a Dog."

1923   Meets Dora Diamant, the young Hassidic girl who will be his companion during the last months of his life. In September moves to Berlin to be with Dora. Intensely involved in Hebrew studies.

1923–1924   In Berlin writes "The Burrow." Health rapidly worsens.

1924   Corrects the proofs of his last collection of stories, *A Hunger Artist,* while very ill in a sanatorium near Vienna. Dies on June 3 and is buried on June 11 in the Jewish Cemetery in Prague-Straschnitz.

Selected Bibliography

Primary Works

Stories Published in Book Form during Kafka's Lifetime

Betrachtung (Meditation). Leipzig: Ernst Rowohlt Verlag, 1913 (printed and copyrighted in 1912). Contains eighteen pieces, most of which had appeared in *Hyperion* in 1908 and in *Bohemia* in 1910: "Kinder auf der Landstrasse" ("Children on a Country Road"); "Entlarvung eines Bauernfängers" ("Unmasking a Confidence Trickster"); "Der plötzliche Spaziergang" ("The Sudden Walk"); "Entschlüsse" ("Resolutions"); "Der Ausflug ins Gebirge" ("Excursion into the Mountains"); "Das Unglück des Junggesellen" ("Bachelor's Ill Luck"); "Der Kaufmann" ("The Tradesman"); "Zerstreutes Hinausschaun" ("Absent-Minded Window-gazing"); "Der Nachhausweg" ("The Way Home"); "Die Vorüberlaufenden" ("Passers-by"); "Der Fahrgast" ("On the Tram"); "Kleider" ("Clothes"); "Die Abweisung" ("Rejection"); "Zum Nachdenken für Herrenreiter" ("Reflections for Gentlemen-Jockeys"); "Das Gassenfenster" ("The Street Window"); "Wunsch, Indianer zu werden" ("The Wish to Be a Red Indian"); "Die Bäume" ("The Trees"); and "Unglücklichsein" ("Unhappiness").

Der Heizer. Ein Fragment (The Stoker. A Fragment). Leipzig: Kurt Wolff Verlag, 1913. Bücherei "Der jüngste Tag," Band 3.

Die Verwandlung (The Metamorphosis). Leipzig: Kurt Wolff Verlag, 1915. Bücherei "Der jüngste Tag," Band 22/23.

Das Urteil. Eine Geschichte (The Judgment. A Story). Leipzig: Kurt Wolff Verlag, 1916. Bücherei "Der jüngste Tag," Band 34.

In der Strafkolonie (In the Penal Colony). Leipzig: Kurt Wolff Verlag, 1919.

Ein Landarzt. Kleine Erzählungen (A Country Doctor). Munich/Leipzig: Kurt Wolff Verlag, 1919. Contains fourteen short pieces: "Der neue Advokat" ("The New Advocate"); "Ein Landarzt" ("A Country Doctor"); "Auf der Galerie" ("Up in the Gallery"); "Ein altes Blatt" ("An Old Manuscript"); "Vor dem Gesetz" ("Before the Law"); "Schakale und Araber" ("Jackals and Arabs"); "Ein Besuch im Bergwerk" ("A Visit to a Mine"); "Das nächste Dorf" ("The Next Village"); "Eine kaiserliche Botschaft" ("An Imperial Message"); "Die Sorge des Hausvaters" ("The Cares of a Family Man"); "Elf Söhne" ("Eleven Sons"); "Ein Brudermord" ("A Fratricide"); "Ein Traum" ("A Dream"); and "Ein Bericht für eine Akademie" ("A Report to an Academy").

Ein Hungerkünstler. Vier Geschichten (A Hunger Artist. Four Stories). Berlin: Verlag Die Schmiede, 1924. Contains "Erstes Leid" ("First Sorrow"); "Eine kleine Frau" ("A Little Woman"); "Ein Hungerkünstler" ("A Hunger Artist"); and "Josefine, die Sängerin oder Das Volk der Mäuse" ("Josephine the Singer, or the Mouse Folk").

Posthumous Collections

Beim Bau der chinesischen Mauer (The Great Wall of China). Afterword by Max Brod and Hans Joachim Schoeps. Berlin: Gustav Kiepenhauer Verlag, 1931; Cologne: Kiepenhauer, 1948. The original edition contained twenty-two pieces: "Beim Bau der chinesischen Mauer" ("The Great Wall of China"); "Zur Frage der Gesetze" ("The Problem of Our Laws"); "Das Stadtwappen" ("The City Coat of Arms"); "Von den Gleichnissen" ("On Parables"); "Die Wahrheit über Sancho Pansa" ("The Truth about Sancho Panza"); "Das Schweigen der Sirenen" ("The Silence of the Sirens"); "Prometheus" ("Prometheus"); "Der Jäger Gracchus" ("The Hunter Gracchus"); "Der Schlag ans Hoftor" ("The Knock at the Manor Gate"); "Eine Kreuzung" ("A Sport"); "Die Brücke" ("The Bridge"); "Kleine Fabel" ("A Little Fable"); "Eine alltägliche Verwirrung" ("A Common Confusion"); "Der Kübelreiter" ("The Bucket Rider"); "Das Ehepaar" ("The Married Couple"); "Der Nachbar" ("My Neighbor"); "Der Bau" ("The Burrow"); "Der Riesenmaulwurf" ("The Giant Mole"), same as "Der Dorfschullehrer"; "Forschungen eines Hundes" ("Investigations of a Dog"); "*Er*" ("He"); and "Betrachtungen über Sünde, Leid, Hoffnung und den wahren Weg" ("Reflections on Sin, Pain, Hope, and the True Way").

Vor dem Gesetz (Before the Law). Afterword by Heinz Politzer. Berlin: Schocken, 1934. Contains "Von den Gleichnissen" ("About Parables"); "Vor dem Gesetz" ("Before the Law"); "Beim Bau der chinesischen Mauer" ("The Great Wall of China"); "Josefine, die Sängerin, oder das Volk der Mäuse" ("Josephine the Singer, or the Mouse Folk"); and "Bericht für eine Akademie" ("A Report to an Academy").

Erzählungen und kleine Prosa (Short Stories and Short Prose Pieces). Berlin: Schocken, 1935; New York: Schocken, 1946; Frankfurt: Fischer, 1952. Contains "Gespräch mit dem Beter" ("Conversation with the Supplicant"); "Gespräch mit dem Betrunkenen" ("Conversation with the Drunken Man"); all the pieces of *Betrachtung (Meditation)*; "Das Urteil" ("The Judgment"); "Die Verwandlung" ("The Metamorphosis"); all the stories of *Ein Landarzt (A Country Doctor)*; "In der Strafkolonie" ("In the

Penal Colony"); all the stories of *Ein Hungerkünstler (A Hunger Artist)*; and "Die erste lange Eisenbahnfahrt" ("The First Long Train Journey").

Beschreibung eines Kampfes. Novellen, Skizzen, Aphorismen aus dem Nachlass (Description of a Struggle). Edited by Ludwig Dietz. Afterword by Max Brod. Prague: Heinrich Mercy Sohn, 1936; New York: Schocken, 1946; Frankfurt: Fischer, 1953; Frankfurt: S. Fischer, 1969. Contains "Beschreibung eines Kampfes" ("Description of a Struggle"); all the stories in *Beim Bau der chinesischen Mauer (The Great Wall of China)*; "Die Abweisung" ("The Refusal"); "Poseidon" ("Poseidon"); "Der Geier" ("The Vulture"); "Der Aufbruch" ("The Departure"); "Gibs auf!" ("Give It Up!"); "Nachts" ("At Night"); "Der Steuermann" ("The Helmsman"); "Der Kreisel" ("The Top"); "Die Prüfung" ("The Test"); "Fürsprecher" ("Advocates"); "Heimkehr" ("Homecoming"); "Gemeinschaft" ("Fellowship"); "Blumfeld, ein älterer Junggeselle" ("Blumfeld, an Elderly Bachelor"); the short play *Der Gruftwächter (The Warden of the Tomb)*; and *Beschreibung eines Kampfes. Die zwei Fassungen Parallelausgabe nach den Handschriften* (Description of a Struggle. The two versions. A parallel edition from the manuscript).

Das Urteil und andere Erzählungen (The Judgment and Other Stories). Frankfurt: Fischer Bücherei, 1952; Frankfurt: Fischer Taschenbuch No. 19, 1975 (37th ed.).

Erzählungen (Short Stories). Frankfurt: Fischer, 1952; Frankfurt: Fischer Bücherei, 1966; Frankfurt: Fischer Taschenbuch No. 756, 1974 (7th ed.).

Hochzeitsvorbereitungen auf dem Lande und andere Prosa aus dem Nachlass (Wedding Preparations in the Country and Other Posthumous Prose). Frankfurt: Fischer, 1953; New York: Schocken, 1953. Contains "Hochzeitsvorbereitungen auf dem Lande" ("Wedding Preparations in the Country"); "Betrachtungen über Sünde, Leid, Hoffnung und den wahren Weg" ("Reflections on Sin, Pain, Hope, and the True Way"); "Die 8 Oktavhefte" ("The Eight Octavo Notebooks"); "Brief an den Vater" ("Letter to His Father"); "Fragmente aus Heften und losen Blättern" ("Fragments from Notebooks and Loose Pages"); "Paralipomena" ("Paralipomena"); and "Rede über die jiddische Sprache" ("Speech on the Yiddish Language").

Erzählungen und Skizzen (Short Stories and Sketches). Edited by Klaus Wagenbach. Darmstadt: Moderner Buch-Club, 1959.

Die kaiserliche Botschaft (The imperial message). Edited by J. Mühlberger. Graz/Vienna: Stiasny-Bücherei, 1960.

Die Erzählungen (The short stories). Edited by Klaus Wagenbach. Frankfurt: Fischer, 1961.

Er (He). Edited by Martin Walser. Afterword by Martin Walser. Frankfurt: Suhrkamp, 1963. An anthology of stories and parables; includes "Brief an den Vater" ("Letter to His Father").

Sämtliche Erzählungen (Collected short stories). Edited by Paul Raabe. Frankfurt: Fischer Bücherei, 1970; Frankfurt: Fischer Taschenbuch, No. 1078, 1975 (10th ed.).

English-Language Collections

The Complete Stories. Edited by Nahum N. Glatzer, New York: Schocken, 1971.

Dearest Father: Stories and Other Writings. Translated by Ernst Kaiser and Eithne Wilkins. New York: Schocken Books, 1954. Contains "Wedding Preparations in the Country," "Reflections on Sin, Suffering, Hope, and the True Way," "The Eight Octavo Notebooks," "Letter to His Father," "Fragments from Notebooks and Loose Pages," and "Paralipomena." *Wedding Preparations in the Country*. London: Secker & Warburg, 1954.

Description of a Struggle. Translated by Tania and James Stern. New York: Schocken Books, 1958. Contains "Description of a Struggle," "Blumfeld, an Elderly Bachelor," "The Warden of the Tomb," "The Refusal," and fifteen short pieces. *Description of a Struggle and the Great Wall of China*. London: Secker & Warburg, 1960.

The Great Wall of China and Other Pieces. Translated by Willa Muir and Edwin Muir. London: Martin Secker, 1933. *The Great Wall of China. Stories and Reflections*. London: Secker & Warburg, 1946; New York: Schocken, 1946. Contains "Investigations of a Dog," "The Burrow," "The Great Wall of China," "The Giant Mole," fifteen short stories, "Aphorisms," "He," and "Reflections on Sin, Pain, Hope, and the True Way."

I Am a Memory Come Alive. Edited by Nahum N. Glatzer. New York: Schocken, 1974. Autobiographical writings.

In the Penal Settlement. Tales and Short Prose Works. London: Secker & Warburg, 1949 and 1972.

The Metamorphosis. A Critical Edition. Edited and translated by Stanley Corngold. New York: Bantam Books, 1972.

Parables (Parabolen). German and English text. Translated by Willa Muir, Edwin Muir, and Clement Greenberg. New York: Schocken, 1947. Enlarged bilingual edition retitled *Parables and Paradoxes*. Edited by Nahum N. Glatzer. New York: Schocken, 1961 (7th printing, 1970); also paperback.

The Penal Colony. Stories and Short Pieces. Translated by Willa Muir and Edwin Muir. New York: Schocken, 1948, 1949; also paperback. *In the Penal Settlement*. Translated by Ernst Kaiser and Eithne Wilkins. London: Secker & Warburg, 1949, 1973.

Selected Short Stories. Translated by Willa Muir and Edwin Muir. New York: The Modern Library, 1952. Contains fifteen short stories.

Wedding Preparations in the Country and Other Posthumous Prose Writings. (Hochzeitsvorbereitungen auf dem Lande). Translated by Ernst Kaiser and Eithne Wilkins. London: Secker & Warburg, 1954; reprinted 1973. Contains "Wedding Preparations in the Country," "The Eight Octavo Notebooks,"

"Letter to His Father," "Fragments from Notebooks and Loose Papers," and "Paralipomena."

Secondary Works

Books

Beck, Evelyn Torton. *Kafka and the Yiddish Theater.* Madison: University of Wisconsin Press, 1971.

Bernheimer, Charles. *Flaubert and Kafka: Studies in Psychopoetic Structure.* New Haven: Yale University Press, 1982.

Brod, Max. *Franz Kafka: A Biography.* Translated by Humphrey G. Roberts and Richard Winston. New York: Schocken Books, 1978.

Carrouges, Michel. *Kafka versus Kafka.* Translated by Emmett Parker. University: University of Alabama Press, 1968.

Corngold, Stanley. *The Commentator's Despair.* Port Washington, N.Y.: Kennikat Press, 1973.

Emrich, Wilhelm. *Franz Kafka. A Critical Study.* Translated by Sheema Zeben Buehne. New York: Frederick Ungar Publishing Co., 1968.

Flores, Angel. *Franz Kafka Today.* Edited by Angel Flores and Homer Swander. New York: Gordian Press, 1977.

Flores, Angel. *The Kafka Problem.* New York: New Directions, 1946; Gordian Press, 1976.

Flores, Angel. *The Problem of "The Judgment."* New York: Gordian Press, 1976.

Goodman, Paul. *Kafka's Prayer.* Introduction by Raymond Rosenthal. New York: Hillstone, 1976.

Gray, Ronald D. *Franz Kafka.* Cambridge: Cambridge University Press, 1973.

Greenberg, Martin. *The Terror of Art: Kafka and Modern Literature.* New York: Basic Books, 1968.

Hamalian, Leo. *Franz Kafka. A Collection of Criticism.* New York: McGraw-Hill, 1974.

Hayman, Ronald. *Kafka: A Biography.* New York: Oxford University Press, 1982.

Heller, Erich. *Franz Kafka.* New York: Viking Press, 1974. Modern Masters series.

Janouch, Gustav. *Conversations with Kafka.* 2nd ed. Translated by Goronwy Rees. 2nd ed. New York: New Directions, 1971.

Kuna, Franz. *Franz Kafka: Literature as Corrective Punishment.* Bloomington: Indiana University Press, 1974.

Pascal, Roy. *Kafka's Narrators: A Study of His Stories and Sketches.* Cambridge and New York: Cambridge University Press, 1982.

Selected Bibliography

Pawel, Ernst. *The Nightmare of Reason: The Life of Franz Kafka*. New York: Farrar, Straus & Giroux, 1984.

Politzer, Heinrich. *Franz Kafka: Parable and Paradox*. Ithaca, N.Y.: Cornell University Press, 1962; expanded edition, 1966.

Rolleston, James. *Kafka's Narrative Theater*. University Park, Pa.: State University Press, 1974.

Sokel, Walter. *Franz Kafka*. New York: Columbia University Press, 1966. Columbia Essays on Modern Writers series, no. 19.

Spann, Meno. *Franz Kafka*. Boston: Twayne Publishers, 1976.

Articles

Beck, Evelyn Torton. "Kafka's Traffic in Women: Gender, Power, and Sexuality." *The Literary Review* 26, no. 4 (Summer 1983):565–76.

Boulby, Mark. "Kafka's End: A Reassessment of 'The Burrow.'" *German Quarterly* 55, no. 2 (March 1982):175–85.

Coetzee, J. M. "Time, Tense and Aspect in Kafka's 'The Burrow.'" *Modern Language Notes* 96, no. 3 (April 1981):556–79.

Cohn, Dorrit. "Kafka's Eternal Present: Narrative Tense in 'Ein Landarzt' and Other First Person Stories." *PMLA* 83 (1968):144–50.

Gelus, Marjorie. "Notes on Kafka's 'Der Bau': Problems with Reality." *Colloquia Germanica* Band 15, no. 1/2 (1982):98–110.

Haase, Donald P. "Kafka's 'Der Jäger Graachus': Fragment or Figment of the Imagination?" *Modern Austrian Literature* 11, no. 3/4 (1978):319–32.

Heller, Peter. "The Autonomy of Despair: An Essay on Kafka." *The Massachusetts Review* 1, no. 2 (February 1960):231–53.

Kauf, Robert. "Once Again–Kafka's 'Report to an Academy.'" *Modern Language Quarterly* 15, no. 4 (December 1954):359–66.

Koelb, Clayton. "'In der Strafkolonie': Kafka and the Scene of Reading," *German Quarterly* 55, no. 4 (November 1982):511–25.

Levine, Robert T. "The Familiar Friend: A Freudian Approach to Kafka's 'The Judgment.'" *Literature and Psychology* 27 (1977):164–73.

Mahlendorf, Ursula R. "Kafka's 'Josephine the Singer or the Mousefolk': Art at the Edge of Nothingness." *Modern Austrian Literature* 11, no. 3/4 (1978):199–242.

Mahony, Patrick. "'A Hunger Artist': Content and Form." *American Imago* 35 (1978):357–74.

McGlathery, James M. "Desire's Persecutions in Kafka's 'Judgement,' 'Metamorphosis,' and 'A Country Doctor.'" *Perspectives on Contemporary Literature* 7 (1981):54–63.

Pasley, Malcolm. "Kafka's Semi-private Games." *Oxford German Studies* 6 (1971):112–31.

Ritter, Naomi. "Art as Spectacle: Kafka and the Circus." *Österreich in Amerikanischer Sicht* 2 (1981):65–70.

Selected Bibliography

Sattler, Emil E. "Kafka's Artist in a Society of Mice." *Germanic Notes* 9, no. 4 (1978):49–53.

Sokel, Walter H. "Kafka's Poetics of the Inner Self." *Modern Austrian Literature* 11, no. 3/4 (1978):37–58.

Spann, Meno. "Don't Hurt the Jackdaw." *Germanic Review* 37, no. 1 (1962):68–78.

Steinberg, Erwin R. "The Judgment in Kafka's 'In the Penal Colony.'" *Journal of Modern Literature* 5 (1976):492–514.

Stockholder, Katherine. "'A Country Doctor': The Narrator as Dreamer." *American Imago* 35 (1978):331–46.

Bibliographies and Research Guides

Beicken, Peter. *Eine kritische Einführung in die Forschung.* Frankfurt: Athenaion, 1974.

Binder, Hartmut. *Kafka-Kommentar zu Sämtlichen Erzählungen.* Munich: Winkler Verlag, 1975.

Caputo-Mayr, Maria Luise and Julius M. Herz. *Franz Kafkas Werke: Eine Bibliographie der Primärliteratur (1908–1980).* Bern and Munich: Franke Verlag, 1982.

Flores, Angel. *A Kafka Bibliography, 1908–1976.* New York: Gordian Press, 1976.

Järv, Harry. *Die Kafka-Literatur: Eine Bibliographie.* Malmö and Lund: Bo Cavefors Verlag, 1961.

Index

Index

The Author

Allen Thiher received his B.A. from the University of Texas in 1963 and his Ph.D. from the University of Wisconsin in 1968. He spent a year in Paris as a Fulbright Scholar and a year in Berlin as a Guggenheim Fellow. He has been a professor of French at the University of Missouri since 1977. He has written articles on modern literature, philosophy, and film, and his books include *Céline, The Novel as Delirium* (1972), *The Cinematic Muse* (1979), *Words in Reflection: Modern Language Theory and Postmodern Fiction* (1984), and *Raymond Queneau* (1985).

The Editor

General editor Gordon Weaver earned his B.A. in English at the University of Wisconsin-Milwaukee in 1961; his M.A. in English at the University of Illinois, where he studied as a Woodrow Wilson Fellow, in 1962; and his Ph.D. in English and creative writing at the University of Denver in 1970. He is the author of several novels, including *Count a Lonely Cadence, Give Him a Stone, Circling Byzantium,* and most recently *The Eight Corners of the World* (Vermont: Chelsea Green Publishing Company, 1988). Many of his numerous short stories are collected in *The Entombed Man of Thule, Such Waltzing Was Not Easy, Getting Serious, Mortality Play,* and *A World Quite Round.* Recognition of his fiction includes the St. Lawrence Award for Fiction (1973), two National Endowment for the Arts Fellowships (1974, 1989), and the O. Henry First Prize (1979). He edited *The American Short Story, 1945–1980: A Critical History.* He is a professor of English at Oklahoma State University and the editor of the *Cimarron Review,* and he serves as an adjunct member of the faculty of the Vermont College Master of Fine Arts Writing Program. Married, and the father of three daughters, he lives in Stillwater, Oklahoma.